THE FLUTE MANUAL

A Comprehensive Text and
Resource Book for Both
the Teacher and the Student

Thomas E. Rainey, Jr.

UNIVERSITY
PRESS OF
AMERICA

LANHAM • NEW YORK • LONDON

Library of Congress Cataloging in Publication Data

Rainey, Thomas E., 1945-
The flute manual.

Bibliography: p.
Includes index.
1. Flute—Instruction and study. I. Title.
MT340.R34   1985   788'.51'071   85-11133
ISBN 0-8191-4776-1 (alk. paper)
ISBN 0-8191-4777-X (pbk. : alk. paper)

All University Press of America books are produced on acid-free
paper which exceeds the minimum standards set by the National
Historical Publications and Records Commission.

DEDICATION

To all musicians who desire to improve both
their flute technique and teaching methods,
I dedicate this book.

iii

ACKNOWLEDGMENTS

It is with the deepest feeling of gratitude that I wish to thank those who have contributed toward the completion of this manual.

A special thanks goes to Dr. Erma Meyerson who provided the necessary guidance and inspiration to complete this text.

Gratitude must also be expressed to the many fine artists whose teaching and performing concepts have knowingly or unknowingly contributed to the contents of this text. Among these are Dante DiThomas, Bernard Goldberg, John Wummer, Joseph Mariano, Marcel Moyse, William Kincaid, Dr. Donald Beikman, Dr. Duane Sample, Mark Thomas, and Dr. Donald McCathren.

Thanks also to photographer Shelle Ramsey.

Finally, a special thanks to my mother, Lyda, for her meticulous professional assistance in the preparation of this text.

vi

TABLE OF CONTENTS

TABLE OF CONTENTS (CONT'D)

PREFACE

Playing and teaching the flute becomes relatively easy once the A B C's of the instrument are understood. This manual is designed to insure that type of learning.

Based upon years of study and research, this book makes available a variety of information on flute technique, teaching suggestions, method books, fingering charts, and illustrations, all of which best meet the needs of teachers and students on all levels of education. A few of these are: the college student preparing for instrumental public school teaching, the applied college flute instructor, the college or high school band and orchestra director, the arranger and composer, the private flute teacher, the public school student, plus the occasional player who simply desires more knowledge concerning the flute.

It is easy to see that this manual is invaluable as both a text and a resource book. By using it, the task of teaching and learning more about the flute becomes both easier and more rewarding.

The best way to do this is to get started.... so let's!

Good Luck,

THE AUTHOR

INTRODUCTION

With the enormous popularity of the flute, comes the tremendous responsibility of teaching it. To assist in this process, the following chapters present concisely the vital information necessary to both play and teach the flute. A brief summary follows.

SECTION I: PREREQUISITES TO FLUTE PLAYING.

Physical Characteristics. Careful selection of students who will play the flute is basic to success. The teacher must see that the students not only have the intellectual capacity but also possess the physical characteristics necessary to properly play the flute. A detailed list of student qualifications is presented to assist in this process.
Selection of Instrument. It is often the responsibility of the educator to assist in the selection of the student's instrument. What models are available, how many extra keys are necessary, and what material flutes are made from are only a few of the topics covered. An understanding of these will help students to make a correct purchase.

SECTION II: GETTING STARTED

After the instrument is purchased, it is time to begin lessons. Educators, often at this point, become in such a hurry to have their students play their first song that they overlook the importance of taking time to insure proper assembly and playing positions. This section focuses on these aspects emphasizing their relevance to the success of the total performer.

Parts. To better acquaint the student with the flute, pictures and descriptions are provided.
Assembling the Instrument. Proper assembly is of utmost importance and must be taught from the very first lesson. Since great damage is frequently done to the flute as a result of incorrect assembly, great detail is provided and a standard procedure given with numerous photographs to assist the educator and student.
Holding the Flute. Incorrect hand and arm positions will greatly reduce the facility of the performer to play rapid passages evenly and quickly. This section covers all aspects of holding and playing positions so that proper placement will be developed from the first lesson.

SECTION III: TONE DEVELOPMENT

Embouchure. Without a well-formed lip position, good
tone production becomes futile. This section explains
ways to develop a good embouchure so that a beautiful
tone can be achieved over the entire range of the
flute.
Tone Development. A better understanding of "how" and
"why" a sound is produced on the flute will increase
the rate of a student's progress. A few of the topics
discussed, basic to this understanding, are the edge
tone concept, velocity and direction of air, and
embouchure flexibility. For the interested reader, a
more detailed account is provided in Appendix A.
Breathing. Beginners are not often taught correct
breathing habits which results in their becoming dizzy,
not being able to sustain passages, or having very
little dynamic control. To assist, steps to correct
breathing are provided and numerous exercises are
given to assist both the instructor and the student.

SECTION IV: DEVELOPING TECHNIQUE

     Eventually, students must strive for complete
command of their instrument. The development of this
control begins with this section.

Tonguing: Discussed and examined is not only the
correct placement of the tongue, but also proper
syllables to use, variations of these syllables, plus
double, triple, and flutter tonguing. Teaching
suggestions are provided for each.
Fingerings. Correct fingerings are also important in
developing technical command. Regular, alternate, trill
and harmonic fingerings are all treated with examples
and teaching suggestions for each.
Intonation. Since many students play out of tune, it
becomes the instructor's job to show the student how to
recognize pitch discrepancies, and what to do to bring
them in tune. To assist, tuning the instrument, correct
cork placement, pitch problem notes, and practice procedures are discussed in detail.
Vibrato. Vibrato, an extremely important technique, is
often never taught resulting in many students developing
it through imitation of other flutists. Since vibrato
can and should be taught, numerous teaching suggestions
and examples are presented.

SECTION V: INSTRUMENT CARE

With the supposition that an instrument can only
sound as good as it plays, proper instrument care
should be emphasized from the first lesson. To help
eliminate damage to a flute resulting from student
abuse, this section discusses daily care, recommended
periodic maintenance, plus a few methods for emergency
repairs.

SECTION VI: FLUTE FAMILY

Since many educators are unaware of the flute
family's numerous functions, this section will bring
about a better understanding of their potential, and
also encourage their use as a more effective means of
education. Ranges, tone production, care and common
problems are only a few of the topics treated.

SECTION VII: APPENDICES

The first six sections of the book are presented
progressively. Additional information significant to
the total understanding of the flute will be found in
the Appendices. The acoustics, history, new trends,
choirs, repertoire, fingering charts, companies that
manufacture flutes, and a list of recommended collateral reading are all included.

The chapters in this book cover every phase of
flute development. By its use, students and teachers
will have a better grasp of what it takes to both
teach and play the flute.

CHAPTER I

PREREQUISITES TO FLUTE PLAYING

Today, educators have become increasingly aware of the need to properly select the right instrument for the right student. One criteria for establishing this selectivity involves a better understanding of the physical characteristics that are advantageous to proper instrument performance.

Consider for a moment the basketball player who has a height advantage over a smaller player. Who is most likely to succeed? Obviously, the taller person will find it much easier to acquire the necessary skills to play basketball and the taller he is, the better his chances of succeeding. This, however, does not mean that the smaller player cannot succeed; it only means that the physical advantage of height is advantageous to his performance as a basketball player.

There are many cases where students desire to play certain instruments but do not possess the necessary physical characteristics to succeed. What do you do? Do you discourage them, recommend another instrument, or give in and let them take lessons on instruments of their choice? Consider the following typical cases:

CASE OF HEART BEING SET ON SPECIFIC INSTRUMENT.

There are many cases where children have their hearts set on a certain instrument and will not consider any other. They have seen a fantastic rock and roll drummer and want to become one, or they want to play the sax simply because their friends do. You, as their instructor, realize that they do not possess the right physical characteristics to play that particular instrument. What do you do?

CASE OF HAND-ME-DOWN.

What about the student who receives a hand-me-down from Grandma's attic, a favorite aunt, a neighbor, or from an older brother. The parents indicate that the student must play this instrument or nothing at all! You judge that it is not the right instrument. What do you do? Do you deprive the child of taking lessons?

CASE OF THE BROKEN-HEARTED GRANDMOTHER.

What about grandma who has been saving her flute for years for her little granddaughter. Finally, the time has come when her grandchild is old enough to begin lessons. She proudly gives her the flute. The little girl brings the flute to school, but you see that she does not possess the right physical characteristics to play the flute. What do you do? Do you break Grandma's heart and tell her that her granddaughter cannot play the flute?

CASE OF THE WASTED MONEY.

There are numerous cases where children obtain instruments from older brothers or sisters who previously took lessons but quit. You judge that physically these are not the best instruments for these students to play, yet, their parents tell you that these are the only instruments they are permitted to play. These parents state that they are not going to waste any more money on instruments when their children may lose interest and quit just as their older brothers and sisters did.

CASE OF THE SWITCH-O-MANIA.

There are many cases where students switch from one instrument to another mainly because they did not possess the right physical characteristics necessary to begin lessons on it in the first place. A classic example involves beginning third or fourth grade clarinet students. After a futile year of attempting to play their instruments and obtain a good sound, many of these students quit or switch instruments. They easily become discouraged when they discover that their fingers are too small to properly cover the holes of the keys. If their hands were bigger, they would not have had to experience this problem. They simply started clarinet lessons before they were physically capable. The question is, why were these students permitted to begin in the first place? Did not their music teachers look for correct hand size? As a result, many of these students quit or end up switching to another instrument.

CASE OF THE DESPERATE MUSIC DIRECTORS.

There are often cases where instrumental directors recommend certain instruments to beginners simply because they have a need for those instruments in their ensemble.

Students are asked to play the tuba, saxophone, or oboe just because of this need while little, if any, consideration is given to determine if the students are physically capable of playing those instruments. There are also instrumental directors who take many of their junior high school players and switch them to other instruments, again, just to fill the void in their instrumentation. Often, using the students' intelligence as the main criteria for playing certain instruments, educators completely forget to check into the physical aspects.

In all the cases above, what would you do? Would you prohibit students to participate? Would you discourage them? Can they adapt so that they can eventually play the instrument? Should students play certain instruments simply because music directors need them? Should students lose out on one of the world's greatest experiences just because they are not allowed to play a specific instrument? The answer, of course, is NO! Something can be done and should be done to help eliminate these concerns. Knowing more about physical characteristics necessary to play certain instruments will help.

The list presented below is representative of characteristics which are advantageous to proper playing and in the majority of cases, are necessary if the student is to succeed. It is almost like the need for teeth to chew food. These physical characteristics definitely contribute to quicker learning and more successful playing, however, if a child lacks in one or two of the areas mentioned on the following pages, it is possible to adapt. If a child does not possess any of these characteristics, it is recommended that the instructor suggest an alternate instrument for study.

PHYSICAL CHARACTERISTICS NECESSARY TO PLAY THE FLUTE

1. Consideration of the arms. It is advantageous for instructors to choose children whose arms are long enough to hold the flute and at the same time cover the keys with their fingers. This can be checked easily by assembling the flute, placing the students' fingers on the keys and helping the students balance their flutes so that the embouchure hole is lined up with their lips. Now, look to see if their arms are too short. If they are, you will notice that the embouchure will be lopsided as shown in Figure 1. A child who has

3

a lopsided embouchure will not be able to produce a proper sound, possibly fall behind the rest of the students and quit.

Figure 1.   Lopsided embouchure.

Another area to check is the little finger of the left hand to see if it reaches the G$\sharp$ key. If a student is unable to reach this key, it often indicates the child is not developed enough (see Figure 2).

Correct   Incorrect

Figure 2. Checking G$\sharp$ key finger.

Remember, some children in the elementary grades are just not developed enough. It may be difficult to discourage them, however, you would be doing them an injustice to have them begin, invest money, and then lose interest because they could not keep up with their peers.

HOW TO ADAPT. It is suggested that students use the 'Head Start Head Joint' built by W. T. Armstrong Company. With this design, the headjoint is curved reducing the distance from the center of the embouchure hole to the first finger position by almost six inches! This makes the flute much easier to handle and easier to play. With this headjoint, students can begin playing the flute as early as age five (see Figure 3). (For a more detailed account, read the educational monograph written by this author and published by W. T. Armstrong Company entitled, "Why the Head Start Head Joint?")

Figure 3. Curved headjoint.

Use of the 'Head Start Head Joint' is ideal, however, if this is not possible, check to see if the school owns any E^b flutes. These are fingered the same as the C flute but are shorter. Students could begin on this shorter instrument and then switch when they grow enough to play the C flute. If the school does not own any E^b flutes, or if the students cannot obtain a 'Head Start Head Joint,' it is suggested that the students wait until they are older to play the flute, or play another instrument.

2. Consideration of the Lips. Lips should, generally, be of smooth texture and not too thick. The basic principle of sound production depends on the suppleness of the lips, thus, having smooth, small lips is a definite advantage (see Figure 4). Unlike other woodwind instruments, the flute does not have a register or octave key to assist in the production of the upper tones. This is basically done with the lips, which further emphasizes the importance of smooth lips.

Consideration, too, should be given to the care of the lips. Many flute students carry with them some form of chap stick which they apply to reduce the chances of obtaining dry, chapped lips. Since this type of situation plays havoc with sound production, it is best to educate students early about lip care and its importance to the production of a proper sound.

Smooth, even lips   Thick, uneven lips

Figure 4. Smooth lips are advantageous.

HOW TO ADAPT. Often, unsuspecting music educators will begin a student who has thick lips and notice good results, then, suddenly, as the range of the flute is expanded, difficulties occur. What can be done to help? The best method is to place the embouchure plate higher on the lower lip. By adapting in this manner, the lower lip will not cover as much of the embouchure hole and a pleasant sound will result (see Figure 5).

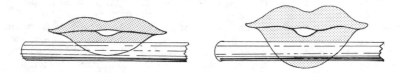

Normal position   Adapting position

Figure 5. Adapting embouchure for thick lips.

3. Tear Drop. Another area to consider in relation to the lip is the tear drop type. In this case, the upper lip has a tendency to have a bead right in the center of it (See Figure 6). Often, educators begin students with this characteristic only to have the students quit after several lessons. What can be done to help? How do you adapt? Since this situation occurs frequently, educators must become aware of the potential problems which develop when students with this type of upper lip formation are permitted to play the flute. To assist

educators so that they will know what to do, the following information is provided.

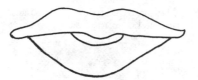

Figure 6. Tear drop.

HOW TO ADAPT. It is recommended that the student with
this type of physical characteristic not play the flute.
Often, the bead in the center of the upper lip drops so
low that it becomes impossible for the student to lift
it enough to properly form an opening for the airstream.
As a result, the bead interferes with the airstream
coming from the player's mouth just enough to split the
air and divide it into two parts. The result is a very
airy, fuzzy tone (see Figure 7).

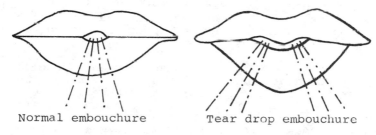

Normal embouchure   Tear drop embouchure

Figure 7. Tear drop affects airstream.

For those who are persistent, it is possible, although not ideal, to adapt by pulling the lower lip to
the left or right of the bead until the desired opening
is achieved. This, of course, means playing off center
or out of the side of the mouth (see Figure 8). With
this type of embouchure, the air will enter the flute
almost centered or at a slight angle depending on the
irregularity of the bead. Also, at times, it is
possible to eliminate the bead by pulling the upper lip
back tightly against the teeth. This helps to bring
the bead in line with the rest of the upper lip allowing
for a more natural opening for the airstream. Having a
tear drop does not mean that a student will not be able
to play the flute, however, there is the possibility

7

that it will become even more of a handicap during the more advanced stages of tone development. Often, a student permitted to take lessons with a pronounced tear drop forms an off-center embouchure to adapt to the problem and seldom achieves any amount of success. Therefore, it is best to suggest another instrument.

Figure 8.   Adjusting to eliminate bead.

4. <u>Consideration of the Teeth</u>. This brings to mind a situation where a little girl runs up to her Dad, sits on his lap, and begins to cry. The little girl's Dad is sensitive enough to know that his little girl is upset, touches her chin gently, and looking into her eyes gives her the warmest, most loving smile a Dad can give to his daughter. She, in return, smiles back revealing a mouth full of braces. Her Dad gave her the confidence to overcome her fear of others laughing at her for wearing braces.

On the elementary level, many students receive some type of dental work. In many cases, braces become a necessity and a concern for both students and educators. Often, educators will be approached by tearful students stating that they must get braces and they ask if they must quit taking lessons. What would you do? What would you recommend?

<u>HOW TO ADAPT</u>. First and foremost is the general rule that teeth which are evenly formed and spaced are an advantage. With this type of physical characteristic, many problems are avoided. Also, all the incisors should be present since these are basic for proper embouchure. Students who do not have incisors should be discouraged until they obtain them.

Secondly, as a general rule, except in extreme cases, a student can wear braces while playing the flute. If, however, the normal playing position feels uncomfortable, it may be helpful to experiment with a lower or higher placement of the embouchure plate on the lower lip. If the lip still hurts, applying a wax to the braces, supplied by the orthodontist, may ease the irritation. Remember, however, whether a student needs braces, or already has them, each case is unique. It is always best to have students confer with their dentists.

Students without braces but with an extreme misalignment of teeth should be discouraged because often this type of dental work involves much more than braces and might become a rather lengthy process.

Students with protruding upper teeth commonly referred to as buck teeth should also be discouraged. These students may find it difficult to properly direct the airstream thereby interfering with good tone production. It is also suggested that those with an excessive overbite or protruding jaw be discouraged. If the student cannot direct the airstream properly, difficulty in tone production will be experienced. An excessive overbite or protruding jaw will interfere with this procedure.

One final point, check to see if students can match their teeth evenly. If they can, this is advantageous and less problems should occur.

5. Consideration of the Lungs. Occasionally, the music educator may encounter a student with very poor lung capacity. They simply cannot hold much air in their lungs. This could be the result of some physical ailment. To properly identify the problem the parents should be consulted. More often than not, this problem can be corrected with proper breathing exercises. Students with a large lung capacity, however, should have a distinct advantage over others in projecting and sustaining a tone. To determine this, ask the student to hold out a note as long as possible on the headjoint. As a general rule, for one breath, 15 seconds is very good for third or fourth graders, and 22 seconds is excellent for fifth and sixth graders. This will increase with practice.

HOW TO ADAPT. If there is a physical problem, check with parent or doctor before discouraging student because playing the instrument may be therapeutic and help eliminate the problem. For others, go over the principles of proper breathing, posture, etc. (See Chapter III).

6. Consideration of Adaptability Classes. Often overlooked is the importance of adaptability classes. These

9

are sessions where students interested in playing the
flute are gathered in a group and are given the basics
in tone production. Usually, they are encouraged to
produce a tone on the headjoint. Normally, after
several sessions, a student is able to produce an even
tone. Those that can will have the advantage over those
who cannot.

HOW TO ADAPT. If a few students cannot produce an even
tone after adaptability classes, this does not mean that
they should quit. Some students are slow starters. It
is recommended that the students be worked with on an
individual basis which, in most cases, remedies the
problem. If, however, no progress is made, possibly
recommend another instrument.

SUMMARY. Remember to consider the above before recommending the flute to an interested student. It is much
better to decide early than to wait and then see many
unhappy children become discouraged and quit because
they did not have the physical capability to play the
flute.

SELECTION OF THE INSTRUMENT

    Once the physical characteristics are checked and
it appears acceptable for the student to play the flute,
it becomes necessary to obtain one. At this point, the
educator may be confronted with a host of questions
such as "Which is the best model to buy?" "How much
does the instrument cost?" "Should the flute be open
or closed hole?" "Is my grandmother's okay to use?"
An educator who cannot answer typical questions such as
these will encounter many embarrassing moments. Consider the following cases.

    There was a student with an intense desire to be-
come an accomplished flutist. After several months of
hard practice and taking lessons at school, little or
no progress was made. The band director suggested
taking private lessons. At the student's first lesson,
a simply overwhelming sight greeted the private instructor. Upon taking a close look at the instrument, the
instructor recognized that the student was taking
lessons on an open G$^\sharp$ key flute, something manufacturers
stopped making years ago. On this model, the pad of the
G$^\sharp$ key is held open by a spring. To close the G$^\sharp$ key,
the little finger of the left hand depresses the key.
Since this key had to remain closed for the majority of
the notes, the little finger was constantly held down

10

restricting the movement of the other fingers on the left hand, especially the ring finger. With the adoption of the closed G$^\#$ key, the reverse occurred. Now, the G$^\#$ key was held closed by a spring and operated by the little finger only when needed giving freedom to the rest of the fingers of the left hand. This improvement is standard today. No wonder the student could not get a sound out. The child was fingering the flute as though it were a closed G$^\#$ key while actually playing an open G$^\#$ key flute. Inquiring where the instrument was purchased revealed the ultimate answer - at a flea market!

The example above is not only upsetting because parents would invest in such an instrument, but also because the music instructor did not recognize the problem thus wasting a great deal of valuable lesson time with the student. Another typical case reveals the following.

A student decided to take private sax lessons because the band director at school claimed that this young aspiring musician could not play in tune. During this student's first private lesson, with a friend of mine, it became evident that the student was playing a C melody saxophone and not an E^b alto sax which is standard today. Unless specified, manufacturers do not make a C melody sax model and, although they look alike, there is no way a C melody sax can play E^b alto sax parts and still play in tune! Upon questioning, the student revealed that the instrument was purchased from a local music dealer who sold it at an inexpensive price because it had been used. As in the flute incident, described above, it is appalling that not only would the music dealer sell such an instrument, but also that the music instructor would not notice it!

Examples such as these are common. In order to avoid similar mistakes, the music educator must be aware of criteria for the proper selection of instruments. Beginning to learn to play an instrument is difficult enough without the added disadvantage of an inferior instrument. If the student already has an instrument, it is up to the instructor to make certain that it is in top playing condition, but if the student does not have an instrument, the music educator must be prepared to recommend one if the parents ask for suggestions.

11

Although there are many ways for students to obtain instruments; for example, grandmother's attic, or a rental program, the main responsibility of the educator is to guide the parent in the right direction and, once the student has the instrument, to make certain that it is in good condition. Remember, good quality instruments should go to beginners. Instruments that do not work properly will cause students to drop out of programs at a faster rate than any other factor.

Since it is not always possible for each student to have the best instrument, the information below should at least help in the process of choosing a more reliable instrument.

1. Don't be afraid to ask the advice of a professional. It is next to impossible to know everything there is to know about every instrument. When in doubt, ask! If an expert is not available, a number of items can be checked to minimize the chance of selecting an unsuitable instrument. A number of these key points will be discussed throughout this chapter.

2. Realize the importance of a new or creditable instrument. Once there were five students taking group lessons on drums. The entire group began with the standard drum pad, sticks, and method book. For the first few weeks, everything proceeded at a normal pace. Then, one day, one of the students appeared with a brand new, shiny, snare drum. The other members of the group stared at this drum in complete awe, probably wishing they had one. Briefly, two things happened over the next few weeks. First, there was no holding back the student with the new snare drum as he progressed at a much faster pace than the other students. On the other hand, three of the remaining four students quit taking lessons. It appeared as though their mental attitude was not as good as that of the student with the new snare drum.

This story illustrates the importance of a new or creditable instrument in giving the student a positive outlook toward achieving success on an instrument. Since the mental attitude appears to improve the student's chance of success, it is important for the music teacher to stress the benefits of a creditable instrument to the parents.

3. Check thoroughly any used instruments students have. Often, students begin lessons on any instrument they

can get their hands on. Educators should inspect these instruments <u>before</u> lessons begin. Taking the necessary time to do this is well worth the effort. Many headaches can be avoided by conscientious educators who discard inadequate instruments <u>before</u> lessons begin. To do this, there are a number of areas that can be checked that will insure a good playing instrument.

a. <u>Make a visual check of the flute</u>. Are there any dents, scratches, bent keys, missing pads, broken springs, bent rods, etc.? If so, this could be an indication that the previous owner did not take very good care of the instrument. In many cases, the price of the repairs does not warrant fixing. Don't be too concerned if the plating is a little worn. This is normal and to be expected. This does not hinder the flute's performance, however, the price should be a little lower as a result of a poorer appearance.

Cases are very important for the flute's performance, therefore, check the case and replace if necessary. The cleaning rod is a very inexpensive item, yet, many students do not have one. Since the rod is important for tuning and cleaning, have students purchase one if it is missing from their cases.

b. <u>Check the 'not-so-obvious' features</u>. Many educators often overlook areas which are extremely important while making an inspection of the flute. These are, however, significant in determining the actual value of the instrument. For instance, does the flute assemble easily? Is the inside of the embouchure hole sharp? Do the pads seat properly? Are the keys in a straight line? Is the spring tension the same on all the keys? To help you determine these aspects, the following information is provided.

First, does the flute assemble easily? Of course the only way to check this is to assemble it. Some flutes are very difficult to put together. This often results in bent keys since students must grab their flutes too firmly in order to assemble them. In addition, there may be a wearing at the tenons due to the friction caused by the joints rubbing together.

13

This increases the chances of air leaking around the tenons which will hinder tone production.

Second, check the inside of the embouchure hole. Make certain that it is sharp and not dulled by a previous owner who may have hit it against something (like a music stand) or may have damaged it by improper cleaning of the instrument. This sharpness is an absolute necessity for proper tone production (see Chapter III). To inspect, place the little finger inside the embouchure hole and, pressing against the edge, turn the finger slightly. A definite sharpness around the edge should be felt on the finger.

Next, check the pads, keys and springs. These are very important mechanical items, thus, great care should be exercised during their inspection. First, depress the keys gently to see if the pads seat (cover the tone holes) evenly. If they don't, they could be worn and should be replaced. If not, air will escape contributing to a poor tone. Also, check to see if the keys close all the way while depressed. If not, there will be a space between the tone hole and the entire pad. This could indicate the adjustment screws need regulated or, possibly, the keys are bent and should be straightened. The keys should also be in a straight line. If not, the pads will not meet the tone holes properly causing air leaks. While checking the keys, notice if the spring tension is the same on all the keys. If not, some keys will be more difficult to press down than others. This can cause unevenness during playing. It is important to remember that the keys must be depressed gently. Pressing the keys down hard only hides the problem, much like taking an aspirin for a headache. Once the aspirin wears off, the headache is still there.

c. <u>Play the instrument</u>. A visual inspection is just not good enough. Playing the instrument is the final test. If possible, (if not, find someone capable) play several scales on the flute so that the entire range of the instrument is heard. Check to see if the instrument sounds in tune or if any of the

tones sound extremely sharp or flat. Does it
appear that all the notes play and sound with
equal ease throughout the range of the instrument? If not, there might be a mechanical
problem or the flute might not be made acoustically correct. (After all, there are some
cars that are lemons, why not some flutes?)

d. Check the manufacturer. Finally, check to see
if the flute was made by a reliable manufacturer. If not, chances for frequent repairs
will result.

4. Understand important new instrument specifications.
Recommending a flute to a potential student is often a
difficult task, however, a better understanding of the
four distinct areas that determine the quality of the
instrument should help in this process. These areas
concern the different models, materials, general workmanship, and extras available for the instrument.

FLUTE MODELS. An educator once related an amusing story
about two concerned parents seeking advice from the high
school band director about the purchase of a new flute
for their fourth grade daughter. The educator, trying
to sound knowledgeable, recommended a Powell flute.
The parents left to purchase one. A short time later,
the parents called the music instructor and told him
to forget about the lessons. The parents were quite
upset claiming there was no way they could spend $2,000
on a flute for their daughter who would, no doubt,
trade it in one day for a baton. Of course, the educator felt foolish recommending something about which he
knew very little, yet instances such as these occur
frequently. Understanding the information which follows
concerning different models of flutes should help eliminate unintelligent recommendations.

a. Professional model flutes. The professional
model flute is usually for the very serious
high school student, college student majoring
in music, or the professional musician. This
does not mean that a beginner could not bene-
fit from using one, but usually its price keeps
most parents from buying it. Companies that
manufacture this model do not make any other
grade of flute. Usually, there is a waiting
list, sometimes a year or more, for those who
desire one. This type of flute is hand-made,
not mass produced, and is of the finest

15

materials. Haynes and Powell are examples of
two companies that manufacture professional
model flutes. Their cost can easily exceed
the amount of $2,000 for a new instrument, how-
ever, because of the demand for such a quality
instrument, they are worth even more in used
condition. Since the professional model flute
is definitely an artist's model, it should con-
tain many of the extras described later in this
chapter.

b. Professional-Student model flutes. There are
companies that manufacture both a professional
and a student model instrument. These companies usually have a fine student model line.
By manufacturing a professional flute, there
is an awareness of the needs of the performer
and many of these features are automatically
incorporated into the student line. As a
result, these instruments need fewer adjustments, are acoustically sound, and are much
better for the beginner. They are manufactured
in a variety of prices ranging from $350 for a
student model to $2,000 for a professional
model. Armstrong, Mateki, Miyazawa, Yamaha,
and Gemeinhardt are a few of the companies that
manufacture such an instrument. It is highly
recommended that parents investigate student
model instruments from this category prior to
purchasing one (see Appendix G).

c. Student model flutes. This type of flute is
the least expensive model. These instruments
are usually manufactured by companies whose
major line of instrument is something other
than flute. An example would be a company
that manufactures a professional model clarinet
or saxophone yet they still manufacture a flute
without making a professional model. Usually,
this type of instrument is not too expensive
but it lacks craftsmanship and numerous adjustments are necessary over a short period of time.

MATERIALS. Another important area to consider when
selecting a flute is the material of which the instrument is made. As a general rule, the denser materials
produce more stability in sound. The player is able
to put more air into the instrument without the sound
seeming forced, therefore, the tone is less likely to
crack. Flutes are made of the following materials:

16

a. Solid silver. Solid silver (either coin or sterling) is considered the most popular among professional flutists. It may be expensive, but produces a beautiful sound.

b. Solid gold (12 or 14K). In this category, there are yellow gold and white gold flutes. Some professionals like the yellow gold because of its warm, mellow sound. Others like the white gold (combination of white gold and nickle silver) for its more brilliant sound. Whatever the preference, its price quickly forces this material out of range for most people, especially students. It is common for those allergic to silver to have their embouchure hole gold-plated to reduce irritation of the skin.

NOTE: By now, the reader of this manual may be thinking that a music teacher should have a medical degree considering that he must know a little about lung capacity, teeth, physical characteristics, etc., and now, allergies! Yet, if only once in the course of a person's teaching career a child is encountered with an allergic reaction and the instructor knows what to do, it is then possible to feel proud and competent as an instructor.

This author recalls a college student who had tremendous potential as a flutist. As a freshman, the student displayed concern over the skin under the lower lip which became sore and irritated after a long practice session. As a high school senior, this student was tempted to quit because of the soreness but, instead, decided to give it one more try on the college level. After a few lessons at college and observation of the infected area, it became apparent that the student was allergic to the flute's solid silver embouchure plate. Shortly after, the student had the embouchure plate gold plated and the problem was solved. This same student became an outstanding flutist, a talent that would have been wasted had the instructor not known what to do.

Generally speaking, if a student is having an allergic reaction to his flute, it

17

is recommended that testing be done to determine what materials he may or may not be allergic to and then plate the embouchure with the proper material.

c. <u>Platinum</u>. Although there are a few flutists who own a platinum flute, it is mainly a novelty flute because of its expense. Some claim that it is too heavy.

d. <u>Nickle plated</u>. Nickle is used to plate a flute made of brass alloy. These flutes are much less expensive than those mentioned above. A nickle-plated flute is very shiny but extremely slippery. This hinders the development of a good hand position as students grasp the flute too firmly or use too much pressure against the lip because of the fear of dropping the flute. For this reason, it is recommended that this material be avoided. However, if a student does have this type of instrument, placing a strip of masking tape where the index finger of the left hand and the thumb of the right hand meet the flute will make the instrument feel more secure and prevent sloppy hand position.

On occasion, the plating on this type of flute may wear off in the areas that contact the skin most frequently. This is usually around the lip plate and where the index finger of the left hand and the thumb of the right hand meet the flute. This is largely due to the extra amount of acid found in the skin of many adolescents. Sometimes a player's lower lip may become irritated when it rubs against an embouchure plate in which the nickle is worn. It is possible to replate this area as well as the entire flute, however it may become so expensive that it would be best to simply invest in a better instrument.

e. <u>Silver plating</u>. This is another type of material used to plate a flute made of brass alloy. Although not a top-line instrument, it does offer an alternative to the nickle-plated flute. This instrument should be recommended for those who cannot afford the more expensive solid sterling silver flute, because of its durability.

18

NOTE: It is possible to combine materials, if desired.
         An example would be a solid silver headjoint
         with a silver-plated body and foot joint. This
         is done to acquire a little better sound while
         it also accommodates the buyer's pocketbook.

GENERAL WORKMANSHIP

    Good craftsmanship is crucial if the instrument is
to play easily and last a long time. The following information will assist educators in becoming more familiar with certain characteristics that are necessary for
a flute to be superbly crafted. (For additional information, read "Selecting a Flute" by Mary Jean Simpson
from which some of the information in this section is
taken. "Copyright 1981 by Instrumentalist Company.
Reprinted from the Instrumentalist, January 1981. Used
by permission.")

    a. Tubing. Since tubing can come in a variety of
        thicknesses, it is best to specify the size
        desired when purchasing a flute. If not, the
        tube will come in a standard size predeter-
        mined by each individual manufacturer. Sizing
        is mostly available on professional models
        while higher costs prevent this type of option
        on student model flutes. Generally, the
        thinner, or lighter, the tubing (.013mm), the
        more brilliant the sound. The thicker, or
        heavier, the tubing (.018mm), the darker the
        sound. This, of course, is a matter of per-
        sonal choice.

    b. Springs. The importance of good quality
        springs is often overlooked when considering
        good craftsmanship. Yet, there is nothing
        more frustrating to a flutist than to have a
        spring break or slip off its hook causing a
        key not to open or close correctly. This
        situation can be easily corrected by using
        springs of good quality and by making certain
        that the springs extend beyond their hooks
        by 1/32nd of an inch. Although springs are
        made from a variety of materials, those made
        from a combination of gold, platinum, and
        palladium are considered the best.

    c. Keys. Before selecting a flute, great care
        must be exercised in observing the keys.
        Keys that are in proper condition will greatly
        increase the ease of playing.

19

First, check to see if the keys are
forged or cast. Forged keys are made by
heating metal until it is ready to be hammered
into shape. This hammering process changes
the molecular structure of the metal in such a
manner that it becomes very strong and durable.
Cast keys are simply made by pouring metal in
a mold until it hardens. This type of key is
much less durable and more apt to bend or
break. Forged keys, therefore, are highly
recommended, especially for the beginner, because of their strength and durability.

Next, educators should become aware of
additional keys which, if properly designed
and built, will make the task of flute playing
somewhat easier. For instance, the two trill
keys (tr^1/tr^2) should be rounded for ease of
playing. Those that are pointed should be
avoided. Because of their size and location,
there is less chance of the fingers slipping
off the trill keys if rounded. Also, make
certain that their height is uniform and
slightly above the surrounding keys.

The D$^\#$ key, however, should not be rounded, but flat in design (see Figure 9). This
will better permit the little finger of the
right hand to both reach the D$^\#$ key and to
assist in a freer motion from key to key on
the foot joint.

Flat   Rounded

Figure 9. Flat D$^\#$ key is best.

Finally, the C$^\#$ key on the foot joint
should be flat. In some of the less expensive models, the C$^\#$ key is the roller type.
A roller, however, impairs the student's
technique because there is less control of
the little finger when moving between the
low C and low C$^\#$ (see Figure 10).

20

Flat C# key   Roller C# key

Figure 10.   Flat C# key.

d. <u>Posts</u>. Check the posts which hold the mecha-
    nism in place. The posts are mounted either
    on ribbing or directly onto the body of the
    flute. It is wiser to invest in a model with
    the posts mounted on ribbing because it will
    be much more durable, thus less likely to
    break (see Figure 11).

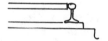 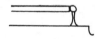

Ribbed mounting.   Direct mounting.

Figure 11.   Ribbed mounting more durable.

e. <u>Tone Holes</u>. Check the construction of the
    tone holes. Tone holes are openings in the
    tube which are closed by the keys. There are
    two types available, those which are integ-
    rally drawn from the body of the flute (rolled
    tone holes), and those which are soldered dir-
    ectly on the tube of the instrument (see
    Figure 12).

Rolled tone hole   Soldered tone hole

Figure 12.   Rolled tone holes best.

    Rolled tone holes are considered the best
for a variety of reasons. First, since rolled
tone holes are drawn directly from the tube,

they are extremely durable with relatively no
chance of breaking off. Soldered tone holes,
however, often deteriorate and frequently
break off causing considerable problems.

Second, rolled tone holes are the same
thickness as the rest of the instrument. This
contributes to a much quicker response than
soldered tone holes which are considerably
thicker and slower in response.

Next, the edges of the rolled tone holes
are rounded while those soldered on are sharper
in design. The smoother edge is much better
since it creates a smoother surface for the key
pad to strike, thus is less likely to damage
the skin of the pad. The sharper edge may
eventually cut into the skins of the pads
causing air leaks, unsatisfactory seating, and
a premature replacement of the pads.

Finally, rolled tone holes are consistently placed at the same location on the tube
while soldered tone holes often vary in placement. The more consistent the placement,
however, the more acoustically in tune the
flute will be. The rolled tone hole flute
offers this feature.

f. Pads. Over the years, various types of pads
have been tried by manufacturers. Those most
practical and durable have been pads made of
skin. These are usually made of felt and
then covered with skin. Pads covered with a
double layer of skin are usually considered
the best. Although skins are made either
yellow or white, the color is not significant.

EXTRAS. There are many options available on the flute.
Investing in a few may be necessary to insure ease of
playing while others are a matter of personal choice.
A few of the more important ones are listed below.

a. Closed G# key. Although the closed G# key has
become standard, manufacturers still provide
the open G# as an option. It is important,
therefore, to specify the closed G# key so that
there will be no mistake upon ordering.

b. Gismo. The gismo (high C^4 facilitator) is
usually added on flutes with a low B key. With

22

the extra tubing necessary for the low B, students often find high C^4 more difficult to play. The use of the gismo makes the high C^4 easier to perform (see Figure 13).

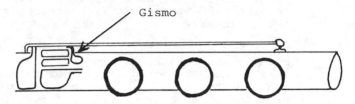

Figure 13. Gismo important with low B.

c. $C^\#$ trill key. The $C^\#$ trill key is located next to the $A^\#$ shake key. When depressed, it opens a $C^\#$ vent located just above the thumb key. This key assists in coordinating the left hand thumb and index finger during rapid B to $C^\#$ trill passages. This key is also helpful in trilling G^3 to A^3 when used in conjunction with the tr^1 key (see Figure 14).

Figure 14. $C^\#$ trill key.

d. B to C trill key. This key is operated by the index finger of the right hand. It replaces the $A^\#$ trill (shake) key. While depressed, it operates the thumb key and is used for trilling from B to C (see Figure 15). It is an option that must be special ordered. It is this author's opinion that this key is of little value and replaces the more important $A^\#$ shake key. This lever should not be ordered unless for a special reason.

B Trill Key

Figure 15. B trill key.

23

e.   Low C$^{\#}$ trill key. This key is operated by the
little finger of the left hand. Since it operates the low C$^{\#}$, a smooth low C to a low C$^{\#}$
trill is possible. This key may be considered
by professionals, however, it is this author's
opinion that it has little practical value for
the beginner.

f.   Split E key. This key is intended to make
high E play easier. It is the judgment of
this author that this key is not necessary
considering the ease of which this note is
produced on today's quality instruments.

g.   Low B key. This key is operated by the little
finger of the right hand. By slightly increasing the length of the flute's tubing, one
more tone is added to the range of the instrument. Often, when students purchase a new
flute, they question the validity of investing
additional money for this key. The advantages
and disadvantages listed below will help educators to properly guide their students. The
final decision, however, should be left to the
individual.

ARGUMENTS FOR:

1.   Many performers prefer a darker tone on
the flute. The added tubing necessary for
a low B adds weight to the instrument
which increases the darkness of the tone.

2.   The added tubing improves the quality of
the upper register, especially C^{4}, which
is a problem area for many performers.

3.   Some performers like to use the low B to
help produce a better high F$^{\#}$ and high B.

4.   Many modern composers are using this note
in their compositions. If a flutist
expects to perform these pieces properly,
this key is necessary.

ARGUMENTS AGAINST:

1.   The balance of the flute becomes changed
because of the extra tubing. (This difference is so slight that it should present
no problem to anyone interested in low B.)

24

2. This key is really not necessary for the majority of flutists who will never play modern literature, especially students.

3. The added expense is not necessary for most public school students who participate in music only during their school years. The low B, therefore, is only for professionals or advanced students who are considering music as a career.

4. This key is not for those who prefer the lighter quality sound over the darker quality.

5. Since the low B key appears only a few times in the literature, it is possible to adapt by either leaving out the note completely, playing it an octave higher, or pulling the mouthpiece out enough so the low B is sounded when low C is played. (This author does not recommend the latter because of the difficulties encountered when the low B is part of a fast passage consisting of several different notes. It would then be impossible to take the time necessary to move the headjoint in or out.)

Remember, the final choice should be left to the individual with consideration given to the above points.

h. Open holes/closed holes. The open hole flute has been a favorite of professionals for years. The open hole model is referred to as the 'French Model' while the closed hole model is called the 'Plateau Model'. Two questions frequently asked by educators are: (1) When did the transition from closed to open keys occur, and (2) Which model is considered the best. The following information will not only make these questions a little easier to understand, but also assist educators in recommending the proper instrument to their students.

TRANSITION FROM CLOSED TO OPEN. Theobald Boehm (see Appendix B) was not only an inventor, but also a fine flutist. As a result, he was better able to understand the needs of the performer and manufactured his instruments to meet these needs. When Boehm completed his flute

25

in 1847, he made a historic change. Prior to
this, flutes were made with all the keys in a
straight line (see Figure 16).

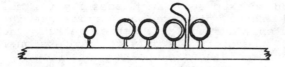

Figure 16.   In line G key.

Boehm thought that the G key should be placed
over to the side where it could be reached more
easily by the ring finger of the left hand.
Boehm thought that this would ease the strain
placed on this finger with the conventional in
line G key flute. Also, Boehm realized that by
placing the key in this position, the fingers
could curve easier assisting the performer in
obtaining the best technique possible. Today's
closed hole flutes have remained virtually the
same without any modifications (see Figure 17).

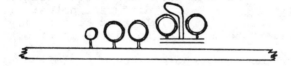

Figure 17.   Offset G key.

Shortly after, Boehm gave a French flute manufacturer permission to build a flute under the
guidance of Louis Lot, a fine French flutist.
The French flutists also had their keys in a
straight line, however, unlike Boehm, decided
not to change the key structure but, instead,
decided to keep them the same and just add the
open keys. The French manufacturers judged
that this would make it much easier for their
customers to adapt. Boehm changed the line of
the keys on his flute for better hand position
while the French firm initially changed to
open keys to make some of their current literature easier to play. This model soon became a
favorite among French flutists, thus, it is
often referred to as the 'French Model'.

WHICH IS BETTER: OPEN OR CLOSED. There are varying opinions on which is better. The following information should assist the student in making the proper choice.

ADVANTAGES:

1. Definitely corrects a sloppy hand position. With the open holes, students must use proper hand position or nothing will come out. Without open keys, the student can easily touch the keys at any point and still get a sound. This develops sloppy hand position which limits smooth technique.

2. The right hand benefits by a correctly placed thumb and little finger (E^b key). This, in turn, gives better balance and permits the fingers to rest properly and relax over the keys. This contributes to better technique. Poor hand position does not allow this to happen.

3. The open hole flute contributes to a slightly more open and brilliant sound thereby improving tone quality.

4. Due to the five open tones, the fingered keys can be set closer to the body allowing shorter travel time which means faster action.

5. There are several fingerings and trills that can be played only on an open hole flute. Too, it is possible to control volume better, tune better, and add different tonal color. These sensitive shadings are possible by half-holing, or venting, the fingerings. To do this, the appropriate key is covered half way. Since the possibilities are so numerous, only a few of the most common and useful half-hole fingerings are presented (see Figure 18).

Figure 18.   Half-hole fingerings.

27

6. Hand size, unless extremely small, should not interfere. There are plugs that go into the keys for those who find it difficult to adapt. These plugs can be gradually taken out one at a time until they are all removed. This aids the student in becoming accustomed to the flute gradually and to develop proper hand position.

DISADVANTAGES:

1. The open hole flute is definitely more expensive. Is this added expense worth it for the average elementary school student? No matter what choice is made, the educator must remember that a prime responsibility is that the student acquires proper hand position.

2. Are harmonics and difficult trills really necessary on the elementary level? Once again, a matter of personal choice, however, this author must admit to not having seen their use on the elementary level.

3. It is difficult to get replacement pads. This is not a very valid reason because this type of pad is standard in most music stores.

4. More delicately constructed. Yes, although this may be true, a student should be able to properly handle an instrument from the very first lesson.

Boehm changed the flute from the in-line to the off-set G key because he thought that this would make it easier for students to acquire good hand position. Yet, many educators use the reasoning that the open hole flute is better than Boehm's because it develops proper hand position while the off-set G key promotes a sloppy one. The open hole flute, however, does not develop but contributes to proper hand position. In other words, it is possible to develop proper hand position on a closed hole flute just as it is on an open hole flute. However, it is impossible to play the open hole flute with incorrect hand position while it is possible to play the closed hole flute with sloppy position.

i. The flute case. One last factor to consider
    is the case. The flute case should be sturdy
    and have strong hinges and latches. This will
    prevent the case from unexpectedly opening
    causing the flute to drop out. This is very
    important, especially for beginners, since
    they have a tendency to be a little careless.
    Too, the case should be well padded and proper-
    ly formed so that the flute will be protected
    and not bounce around while being carried or
    placed down. It is also helpful to have an
    insulated cover that zips up and fits over the
    flute case. This will help protect the flute
    from drastic temperature changes.

    NOTE: It is strongly suggested to visit a
    flute manufacturing company to witness the
    making of a flute. This will assist the edu-
    cator in becoming even more familiar with the
    different options available and provide more
    insight concerning the information presented
    above.

CHAPTER II

GETTING STARTED

PARTS OF THE INSTRUMENT

FLUTE PARTS. Once the student obtains the flute, it
becomes necessary to learn the names of the different
parts (see Figure 19). Acquiring this terminology
would not only aid the instructor while teaching the
various aspects of flute assembly, but also provide a
reference point while teaching instrument care, holding
positions, and flute maintenance.

NOTE: Some used instruments may have protective caps
which are put on the tenons of the flute while it is
in the case. These are obsolete. They were initially
used to prevent damage to the connecting tenon. Frequently, however, these caps create friction at the
joint which causes a wearing down and an improper fit.
If students have them, throw them away.

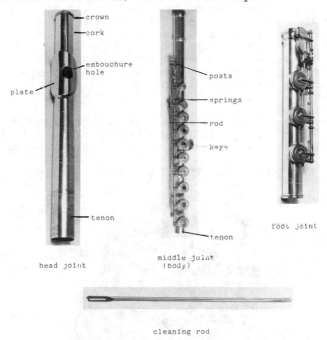

Figure 19. Parts of the flute.

ASSEMBLING THE FLUTE

ASSEMBLING. After students acquire the proper terminology concerning the parts of the flute, the next step is to assemble their instrument. Proper assembling is a necessary skill to acquire from the very first lesson. Students who neglect to do this often damage their instruments and lose valuable lesson and practice time while they wait for them to be repaired. Consider the following typical example:

> Susan and Mary begin lessons at the same time. They both go home to practice their assignment. Mary, being a little careless, assembles her flute incorrectly and damages one of its keys. As a result, Mary's flute leaks air resulting in a poor tone. Mary assumes that her difficulties are normal for a beginner. The next week, both students attend their lesson. Susan knows her lesson while Mary is still experiencing problems. As the music instructor attempts to figure out Mary's problem, he notices a bent key on her flute. The instructor then notifies Mary that she must have her instrument repaired. Mary proceeds to do this, yet, by the time Mary gets the flute to the repair shop and back, she has already missed three or more lessons! Susan is already on her fourth lesson while Mary is still just beginning!!

Thus, the importance of proper assembling is crucial from the very beginning. Although there are different ways of doing this, the following has proven successful.

STEP 1. Take the headjoint out of the case (see Figure 20).

Figure 20. Proper way.

32

STEP 2. Place the headjoint in the left hand making certain that the fingers grasp it below the embouchure plate because this plate is soldered on and can come off with abuse (see Figure 21).

STEP 3. Take the body (middle joint) in the right hand. Avoid grasping the mechanism in order to prevent damage to the keys and rods (see Figure 22).

Figure 21. Take the headjoint in the left hand.

Figure 22. Take the body in the right hand.

STEP 4. Connect the body with the headjoint using a slight twisting motion (see Figure 23).

Figure 23. Connect body with headjoint.

Emphasis should be placed on the twisting motion to avoid the possibility of students forcing these sections together. Pushing the joints straight in creates friction which, in turn, causes eventual wear around the joints. When this occurs, the joints do not fit snugly causing air leaks, misalignment of the headjoint with the body, and in some cases, the headjoint slipping off

33

the flute which causes further damage. Remember, use a twisting not a pushing motion.

STEP 5. Align the headjoint with the middle joint. There are several ways to do this. Some student flutes have one line on the headjoint and several lines on the middle joint (see Figure 24).

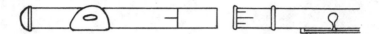

Figure 24. Guide lines for proper alignment.

On this type of flute, line up the center line (the longest line) on the middle joint with the single line on the headjoint (see Figure 25). This is usually the best position for beginners.

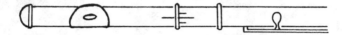

Figure 25. Best guide line
position for beginners.

If the above position is not satisfactory, move the headjoint to line up with one of the other lines on the middle joint until satisfactory results are obtained (see Figure 26).

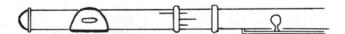

Figure 26. Alternate guide
line positions.

Under no condition should the flute be lined up beyond this point since a lopsided embouchure will develop (see Figure 27).

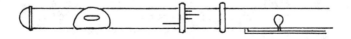

Figure 27. Incorrect guide line position.

34

If the flute does not have lines to assist in the
proper alignment, line up the embouchure with the C
hole on the middle joint. This is the first key on
the body (see Figure 28).

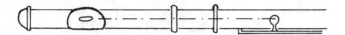

Figure 28. Proper alignment
without guide lines.

Although being able to line up the flute without guidelines is the best, it may prove too difficult for some
beginners. Some educators recommend putting some type
of scratch on each section to assist the student in
lining up the flute. This author sees no value in this
method other than scratching and damaging the flute. A
better method is to place masking tape on each section
not only making it much easier for the student to see,
but also, after the student acquires the proper technique, the masking tape can be removed with the flute
having a new appearance than with a scratch on it (see
Figure 29).

Figure 29. Alternate method of
aligning flute without guide lines.

The purpose for properly aligning the headjoint is two
fold. First, incorrect alignment causes incorrect hand
position. This unnatural position of the hands affects
the free movement of the fingers causing sloppy technique. Secondly, incorrect alignment causes a poor
embouchure. This often limits the student's ability to
produce a pure flute tone.

STEP 6. Next, grasp the foot joint attempting to avoid
the keys and mechanism (see Figure 30).

Figure 30. Grasp foot joint.

STEP 7. Take the body of the flute. Grasp it with either hand once again avoiding mechanism (See Figure 31).

RIGHT HAND   LEFT HAND

Figure 31. Grasp body of the flute.

Once again, for reasons stated in Step 4, use a twisting motion to connect the two joints. Notice how the hands avoid the mechanism (see Figure 32).

Figure 32. Connect the body
to the foot joint.

STEP 8. Make certain that the foot joint and the middle joint are properly aligned. To do this, line up the mechanism rod on the front joint with the center of the D key on the middle joint which is the last key on the body (see Figure 33).

Figure 33. Correct alignment of the foot joint.

36

A common error for beginners is to line up these two
sections rod to rod (see Figure 34).

Figure 34.   Incorrect alignment
of foot joint.

This should be checked continually because incorrect
alignment will result in poor position of the little
finger of the right hand. By lining up these two
sections properly, the three keys on the foot joint are
put in the best position for the little finger to
operate them most naturally.

SUMMARY. Although there are many methods of assembling
the flute, depending on the preference of the teacher,
there is still one very important rule that is common
to all procedures, namely, no pressure should be put on
the keys or rods during assembly. Avoid grasping the
mechanism whenever possible. The procedure mentioned
above is a safe one for the beginner because it follows
this principle. Following these guidelines will insure
a properly assembled flute (see Figure 35).

Figure 35.   A properly assembled flute.

HOLDING THE FLUTE

PROPER HAND POSITION. After the student learns how to
assemble the flute, the next step is to develop proper
hand position. Since the flute has the unenviable dis-
tinction of being the only member of the woodwind family that is held transversely, the beginning student
cannot see his fingers, usually feels insecure, grabs
the flute any way possible, and limits the muscular
freedom necessary to adequately move the fingers (see
Figure 36).

Figure 36. The flute is held
in a transverse position.

Close supervision is crucial at this stage of development. The instructor must give adequate attention to
and insist that the student use the correct hand
position from the very first lesson. The rate of progress can be facilitated by correct position so contin-
ual checks must be made by both the student and the
instructor.

To assist in this process, the following basic principles are provided. Allowances can be made for individual physical differences, however, as in sports, the
better the form, the better the athlete. The following
is considered the best form for the flutist.

LEFT HAND POSITION

STEP 1. First, take the body of the flute and rest it
at the base of the index finger between the knuckle and
the first joint. Place the index finger near the C key
in such a manner that the rest of the keys can be
reached by the other fingers (see Figure 37). This will
help establish the correct contact point.

Figure 37. Correct placement of index finger.

STEP 2. The thumb should be placed on the B key at a slight angle (see Figure 38). Placing too much thumb on the key restricts movement of the rest of the hand (see Figure 39).

Correct

Incorrect

Figure 38. Correct place-
ment of right hand thumb.

Figure 39. Incorrect
placement of right
hand thumb.

STEP 3. Next, place the remaining fingers on the keys. Remember to skip one key between the index finger and the middle finger since beginners have a problem with this (see Figure 40).

Figure 40. Correct placement of
remaining left hand fingers.

Also, notice the curve of the fingers. The index finger has a rather large curve with each succeeding finger having less and less, down to the little finger which has hardly any curve (see Figure 41). Many beginners use too much pressure on the keys, thus restricting the movement of the fingers. Normally, when this occurs, the second and third fingers will appear too flat (see Figure 42). This must be corrected at once.

Figure 41. Correct curve of fingers of left hand.

Figure 42. Incorrect curve of left hand fingers.

STEP 4. Pay particular attention that the little finger touches or remains slightly above the $G^\#$ key while not in use (see Figure 43). Make certain the student does not tuck it under the key (see Figure 44). This is a common problem that restricts the free movement of the other fingers.

Figure 43. Correct placement of left hand, little finger.

Figure 44. Tucking the little finger under the $G^\#$ key.

RIGHT HAND POSITION

STEP 1. In addition to the index finger of the left
hand, the right thumb helps balance the body of the
flute. Correct placement is important. To achieve
this, the thumb should be placed under the F key (see
Figure 45).

Figure 45. Correct position of right thumb.

STEP 2. The rest of the fingers should be brought to
the center of the keys (see Figure 46). Make certain
that the fingers do not overlap the mechanism (see
Figure 47). Educators should be sensitive to this from
the beginning. Sloppy hand positions produce sloppy
technique. Fingers that extend too far can best be
corrected by bringing the thumb further back.

Figure 46. Correct position   Figure 47. Incorrect
of right hand.   position of right hand.

STEP 3. The student should use the balls or flat parts
of their fingers to depress the keys (see Figure 46).
Students should never use the tips of their fingers
since this leads to sloppy playing (see Figure 48).

Figure 48. Never use tips of fingers.

STEP 4. Next, the little finger depresses the E^b key
(see Figure 49). Since this finger is down on all but
four notes in the normal playing range, it, too, helps
balance the flute.

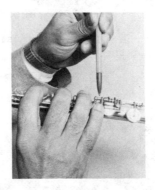

Figure 49. Correct position
of little finger.

Students should realize that the little finger is not
straight but, instead, curved a little while depressing
the E^b key. It begins, however, to gradually straighten
out as it depresses the C and C$^\sharp$ keys. It becomes
quite straight if the flute has a low B key. This is
important to consider because keeping the finger curved
for all keys will hinder technical fluency.

SUMMARY. The importance of proper hand position cannot be overemphasized. Close supervision by the instructor is imperative not only at the beginning steps, but throughout the student's career.

OTHER POINTS TO CONSIDER.

POINT 1. There should be a "U" shape between the thumbs and the index fingers of both hands (see Figure 50). Proper "U" shape is important in order to curve the fingers properly so that they are in a natural position allowing for maximum freedom of movement. If a student has difficulty achieving this shape, simply move the thumb of the right hand, or the index finger of the left hand, up or down the flute until the desired shape is formed.

Figure 50. Correct "U" shape.

POINT 2. The wrists should be flat, not up in the air (see Figure 51).

Wrist too high   Correct wrists

Figure 51. Watch wrist position.

43

POINT 3. Fingers should be no more than one inch above the keys (see Figure 52). If they are too high, it slows down the action (see Figure 52).

Correct height of
fingers

Incorrect height of
fingers

Figure 52. Watch height of fingers
above keys.

POINT 4. Remember the three points of balance. Since the weight of the instrument is supported at these points, they should be constantly checked. These areas are: the lips, index finger of the left hand, and the thumb of the right hand (see Figure 53).

Figure 53. Points of balance.

Since the little finger of the right hand is often depressing the D# key, it is sometimes thought of as a
fourth point of balance. This author prefers not to
think of the little finger of the right hand as such
because with the balance points properly positioned and
no fingers down, it is possible to play a note without
dropping the flute. However, without any one of the
other balance points positioned properly or making
contact at all, the flute will easily drop. The little
finger of the right hand adds more support to the
already existing balance points. A good procedure to
use in checking proper position of these points of
balance is to have the student play a note without depressing any of the keys. Watch to see if the flute
slips or the student has to grab to insure the flute
not dropping. If this occurs, correct immediately.

PROPER STANDING POSITION

Another aspect to consider is the correct position for
holding the flute while standing. A student neglecting
this area can further impede his progress, while proper
execution will enhance it. Although there might be
slight deviations, the suggestions below are almost
unanimously accepted as correct for the majority of
flutists.

POINT 1. Make certain the flute is in the correct horizontal angle with the body. Generally, there is a
slight downward sloping to the player's right. Specif-
ically, this slant should be fifteen to twenty degrees
(see Figure 54). Beginners sometimes have the tendency
to angle the flute too high, too low, or too level.
Watch for these signs and correct at once.

Figure 54. Correct horizontal angle.

45

POINT 2. Make certain the flute is in the correct
vertical angle with the body (see Figure 55). Frequently, beginning students pull in (see Figure 56) or
push the flute out too far (see Figure 57). Correct
immediately before bad habits develop.

Figure 55. Correct vertical
angle.

Figure 56. Vertical
angle too far in.

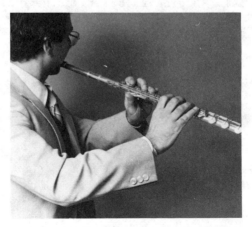

Figure 57. Vertical angle too far out.

POINT 3. Make certain the head is tilted to follow the line of the flute (see Figure 58). This is crucial since tilting the flute, but not the head, leads to incorrect embouchure, subsequently, a poor tone (see Figure 59).

Figure 58.   Correct tilt of head with flute.

Figure 59.   Incorrect tilt of head with flute.

POINT 4. Make certain shoulders are tilted to follow the line of the flute (see Figure 60).

Figure 60.   Correct tilt of shoulders.

POINT 5.   Make certain the elbows are free from the
body.   Beginners have a tendency to tuck them in too
far which restricts proper breathing.

POINT 6.   Make certain the flute does not rest on the
shoulder.   Beginners, in order to feel more secure,
rest the headjoint on the shoulder.   This should be
corrected immediately.

POINT 7.   Make certain the student stands with feet
slightly apart.   One foot should be ahead of the other
to help maintain balance.

POINT 8.   Make certain the head remains up.   Often
beginners tuck their heads down for added security.

SEATED POSITION

The position of the instrument in the seated position
is identical with that of the standing position.   The
only change is the position of the body.

POINT 1.   Make certain feet are flat on the floor, no
feet on the back of the chair, no legs crossed, etc.

POINT 2.   Body must be erect and seated slightly forward away from back of chair (see Figure 61).

Figure 61.   Proper seated position.

POINT 3.   One further word about chairs.   A common
problem for band directors is what to do with all those
flute players in an already crowded practice room.
Often students resort to all types of positions just to
squeeze their flutes in.   Figure 62 provides an example
of a common occurrence (see Figure 62).

Figure 62.   Incorrect seated position.

This type of posture does nothing but develop bad
breathing habits and sloppy technique.   A simple
solution is to alternate the chairs so that one is up
and the other back.   By doing this, the line of the

flute will be directly in front of or behind the adjacent flutist and proper holding position can be achieved (see Figure 63).

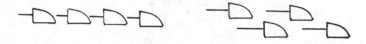

Incorrect   Correct

Figure 63.   Suggested seating arrangement.

If the band room is too small to move the chairs in this manner, it is suggested to use the Head Start Headjoint (see Chapter I). By using the curved headjoint, this problem is eliminated while still giving the students enough room to properly hold their flutes.

OTHER FACTORS TO CONSIDER

POINT 1. When seated and resting flute on lap, always keep keys up to prevent pads from absorbing a lot of the moisture produced by playing the flute (see Figure 64).

Figure 64.   Proper rest position.

POINT 2. When using a music stand, always position it so that the head does not tilt downward (See Figure 65).

Figure 65.   Normal stand position.

POINT 3.   Body posture should be good.   There should be no slouching.

POINT 4.   Check for excessive body movements.   A child moving all over his seat cannot possibly be emotionally involved in whole notes!   Although some movement may be desirable at a later stage of development, for the beginner, it can only hinder his progress.

POINT 5.   Use a mirror.   Students will be surprised at how much they can learn simply by looking at themselves while practicing.

POINT 6.   Have students think of the flute as being balanced rather than being held.   With other instruments, the mouth plays a definite role in the support of holding the instrument.   With the flute, however, the instrument rests on the lip.

SUMMARY.   From reading the above, it becomes apparent that proper holding position is both necessary and important to learn from the first lesson.   Since the holding position for the flute is basically set, the positions illustrated should be kept at all times. Educators should constantly check these positions until they become automatic.

REMEMBER, THERE SHOULD BE NO EXCUSE FOR A POOR HOLDING POSITION EITHER STANDING OR SITTING.

CHAPTER III

TONE PRODUCTION

EMBOUCHURE

EMBOUCHURE. Developing a good flute tone is often one of the most elusive parts of flute playing. Unlike the other woodwind instruments which have vibrating reeds to assist in tone production, the flute must rely solely on the physical control of the player's mouth. This means that a student must have an accurate embouchure to produce a true flute sound. A student can possess all the technique in the world, but without a good sound, this is meaningless. Great care must be taken to insure an understanding of embouchure and its relationship to tone production. The following is intended to assist in this process.

EMBOUCHURE FORMATION. Embouchure may be defined as the formation of the lips in a correct manner to produce a proper tone. Other surrounding physical factors which affect tone production are also part of a correct embouchure. These are the chin, the jaw, the tongue, and the bony structure of the face (see Figure 66).

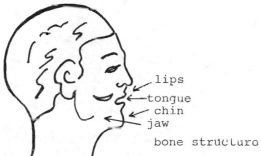

lips
tongue
chin
jaw

bone structure

Figure 66. Factors affecting correct embouchure.

It is important to realize at this point that although there may be differences in the students' outward appearances and physical characteristics in regard to the above, there is still one basic concept that should be taught that is inherent in all flute embouchures. An approach that has proven successful follows. Proper embouchure placement should occur if these steps are taken.

STEP 1. USE THE HEADJOINT ONLY. This is the only section that should be used until the embouchure is set
(see Figure 67). This will make it much easier for the
student to concentrate on embouchure without the added
worry of holding the entire flute.

Figure 67. Use headjoint only.

STEP 2. MAKE CERTAIN THE STUDENTS' LIPS ARE RELAXED AND
CLOSED. Some educators refer to this position as a
"natural smile". The smile gives just enough firmness
at the corners of the mouth to form a good embouchure
and, at the same time, allow enough looseness for the
flexibility needed to develop a good tone (see
Figure 68).

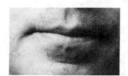

Figure 68. Lips should be
relaxed and closed.

STEP 3. PLACE FLUTE HEADJOINT TO LOWER LIP. The lip
plate should rest in the curve of the chin just below
the lips (see Figure 69).

Front View   Side View
Figure 69. Rest mouthpiece in curve of chin.

54

STEP 4. MAKE CERTAIN THE HEADJOINT IS PARALLEL WITH THE
LINE OF THE LIPS (see Figure 70).

Figure 70. Headjoint is parallel
with line of lips.

STEP 5. CENTER THE FLUTE. This is important so that
the embouchure hole is not too far to the left or right
of the opening in the lips. An off-centered embouchure
will produce a very airy sound (see Figure 71). Centering the flute properly will eliminate this problem. To
center the flute, roll the mouthpiece in until the hole
is centered flatly on the lips. This is called "kissing
the flute" (see Figure 72).

 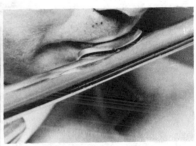

Figure 71. Embouchure   Figure 72. Centering
not centered.   flute.

Once this is done, roll the flute back out and the
mouthpiece should be properly centered (see Figure 73).

Figure 73. Roll flute out.

STEP 6. COVER THE PROPER AMOUNT OF EMBOUCHURE HOLE
WITH THE LOWER LIP (see Figure 74).

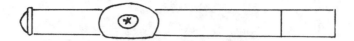

Figure 74.   *Embouchure hole which
will be partly covered by lower lip.

Although this is an individual matter, generally the
sharp inner edge of the mouthpiece rests firmly on the
base of the lower lip (see Figure 75). This point of
contact is constant and should never be altered by the
beginner while playing the flute. Normally, for most
students, this point of contact occurs where the bottom
portion of the lower lip meets the skin immediately beneath it. This step should be carefully supervised by
the educator to insure proper embouchure development.

Figure 75.   Base of lower lip
where flute rests.

Normally, the lower lip should cover 1/4 to 1/3 of the
inner part of the embouchure hole. The rest of the
outer edge of the embouchure hole should remain open
(see Figure 76).

Figure 76.   Normal lip covering.

If too much is covered, a flat airy sound will result
(see Figure 77). If too little is covered, a sharp,
airy, thick sound will result (see Figure 78).

56

Figure 77. Too much
covering.

Figure 78. Too little
covering

The correct covering should appear as shown in Figure 79
(see Figure 79).

Figure 79. Correct embouchure
hole covering.

STEP 7. POSITION OF THE LIPS. Once the lips are centered and the correct amount of embouchure hole is
covered, the next step is to form the correct lip
position (see Figure 80). To do this, try pulling the
corners of the mouth slightly back, almost in the
manner of a "natural smile" (see Step 2). This should
help to correctly position the lips.

Figure 80. "Natural smile" position.

If the "natural smile" concept does not help, try another approach. A good method is to have the students
form their lips as though they were saying the word
"pee". Say it and see how it pulls the lips back (see
Figure 81). Syllables such as "poo" are a no-no!!
They definitely form an incorrect shape for the lips
(see Figure 82). Say "pee" and "poo" and see the
difference.

Figure 81. "Pee" shape.   Figure 82. "Poo" shape.

STEP 8. PRODUCING THE FIRST TONE. To produce the first
sound, take the headjoint in the left hand and cover the
open end with the palm of the right hand (see Figure 83).
Place the headjoint to the lips in the manner described
in the first seven steps.

Figure 83. Place closed headjoint to lips.

Open the lips slightly and release a small amount of
air. The sound produced will be an A which is the fundamental tone, an octave below the tone of the open
headjoint (see Figure 84).

Closed   Open

Figure 84. First tones produced on
a closed and open headjoint.

The correct shape opening at this point should be oval
and the size should be approximately 3/8 of an inch long
and 1/32 of an inch wide (see Figure 85).

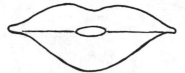

Figure 85. Correct shape of
lip opening.

STEP 9. MAKE CERTAIN CORRECT AMOUNT OF AIR IS RELEASED.
Students, at this point, may become dizzy from blowing
too hard. Many educators advise their students to rest
a few minutes before trying again. Although this is
safe advice, it does not solve the problem. Something
that may help is an understanding of the "cool air"
versus the "hot air" concept. To demonstrate, have
students blow a cool stream of air on the palm of their
hands. To do this, students must pull their lips back
slightly as if saying "pee" and emit a concentrated
stream of air (see Figure 86).

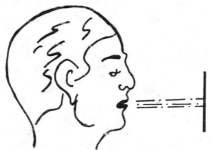

Figure 86. "Cool air" concept.

To produce the "hot air" concept, simply have students
open their mouths wider and emit air into palm of hand
as if saying "haah". Warm air should be felt (see
Figure 87).

Figure 87.   "Hot air" concept.

The flute uses the "cool air" concept while the saxophone uses the "hot air" principle. If flute students try to obtain a sound by using the "hot air" principle, they will soon become dizzy. This results from using air at a quicker rate of speed than necessary to produce a sound on the flute. Cool air must be used for the flute.

There are many methods of teaching this concept. A few of these are listed below:

a. Spoonful of soup method. Ask students to demonstrate how they would cool off a spoonful of soup. Think about this for a minute. The only natural way to do this is to form the lips so that a small, cool, centered stream of air is emitted. If this is not done, too much air will come out causing the soup to spill. Have students try this with a spoonful of water.

b. Feather method. Students should try to keep a feather in the air by forming an embouchure and emitting air. If students resort to a "poo" shape, they will notice what little control they have over the feather and how quickly it will fall to the floor. Students who use the "pee" shape will discover that the feather will remain in the air much longer as a result of a more concentrated air stream.

c. Soda straw method. To develop a better idea of the correct cool air embouchure formation, have students insert a soda straw into their mouths. Ask them to keep their lips together firmly, but not too tense, and then remove the straw. Ask students to keep their lips in the same contour as if the soda straw were still there. Cool air should result upon emitting air.

STEP 10. PRODUCING A SECOND TONE. After practicing the A on the closed headjoint and concentrating on the cool air concept, students should be ready to try another note. Achieving this second note is crucial not only to the development of proper embouchure, but also to the basic principle of sound production on the flute. This new sound will be a high E, a twelfth higher than the A (see Figure 88).

Figure 88. Producing two notes
on the closed headjoint.

To produce this sound, students must make the embouchure
hole smaller, emit less air, and change the direction of
the air so less air enters the flute. This may sound
confusing yet it is relatively simple and must be acquired if proper tone production is desired. The following suggestions are provided to assist in this process.

a.   Direct a cool stream of air directly on the
     center of the palm of the hand (see Step 9).
     Now move the lower lip up (out) and down (in)
     a number of times. Notice how air coming from
     the mouth travels up and down the palm of the
     hand (see Figures 89 and 90). Sometimes stu-
     dents understand this concept easier if the
     term jaw is used instead of lip. (This author,
     however, prefers using the term lip.) Through-
     out this process, educators should make certain
     that their students are using the "pee" shape
     embouchure or this exercise will be futile.

Figure 89. Directing air   Figure 90. Directing
down.   air up.

b.   Now, take the headjoint, close the open end,
     and play the low A notated in Figure 88 (see
     Figure 88). After the sound is produced, move
     the lower lip up and out so that less air
     enters the flute. A high E should result (see
     Figure 88). A mistake some students make is to
     blow harder until the high sound comes out.

This is wrong! It is very important for students to understand that the same amount of air must be used on the high E as with the low A. It is the lower lip that does all the necessary work by changing the direction of the air so that less air enters the flute. Remember, is is <u>less</u> air entering the flute that produces a <u>higher</u> sound, not <u>more</u> air.

Another mistake some students make is to turn their headjoints in towards their lips until a higher sound is produced. In essence, what they are doing is creating a situation where it is impossible to get more air into the flute. As the headjoint opening is turned towards the lips, the air travels out and over the embouchure hole. Thus, less air enters the flute and a higher sound is produced. This method is totally inadequate and should be discouraged from its first occurrence. The sound produced will be muffled and out of tune.

c. It is extremely important at this point for the students to understand this concept: the <u>higher</u> the sound the <u>less air</u> into the flute, and the <u>lower</u> the sound, the <u>more air</u> into the flute. The lower lip assists in this process.

d. Also assisting in this process is the size and shape of the opening in the lips. The wider, more oval the shape of the lips, the larger the amount of air able to enter the flute (see Figure 91). Therefore, since the lower register needs more air into the instrument to produce the best sound, the lower lip is dropped down and at the same time, the opening becomes wider in the lips. For the higher register, the opposite is true. Since less air is needed for the higher register, the lower lip moves out (up) and the opening becomes smaller to produce the best sound.

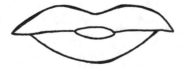

Figure 91. Lip opening for lower register.

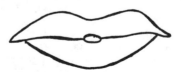

Figure 92. Lip opening for upper register.

e. Students should practice these two tones (see Figure 88) numerous times without tonguing (slurring) to make certain that the correct principle is understood. Lip flexibility is of utmost importance for proper sound production. By achieving this knowledge prior to putting the instrument together saves a large amount of learning time.

SUMMARY. The three basic dimensions of the embouchure which control the sound are its size, shape and angle. The size determines how much air can be emitted, the shape determines how the air will be centered, and the angle determines which direction the air travels. Combining the above will assist the students in using the embouchure for its maximum use, namely, producing a pure tone.

NOTE: CAUSES OF POOR TONES FOR BEGINNERS. Often beginners experience problems that should be corrected at early stages to minimize the possibility of developing bad habits that hinder the rate of progress. A few of the common ones and suggested remedies are listed below.

1. Very small, muffled or choked sound....flute turned in too far. Turn out to normal position.

2. Open, fuzzy sharp sound....flute turned out too far. Turn in to normal position.

3. Breathy sound....air is not centered over embouchure hole. Shift flute mouthpiece to left or right until air is centered.

4. Loud, rough sound....blowing too hard, forcing sound. Go over cool-air concept.

5. Notes drop to a lower pitch while trying to play a higher one....not changing direction of air. Must develop a more flexible lip. Practice on closed headjoint low A to E.

6. Weak sound....check for leaky instrument.

7. Tight, thin sound with no flexibility....mouthpiece placed too high on lower lip. Move down to where the bottom portion of lower lip meets the skin immediately beneath it.

8. Very sharp, but embouchure okay....lips too tight at corners. Loosen lips slightly.

9. Very flat sound....not enough firmness at corners. Tighten up slightly.

TONE DEVELOPMENT THROUGH ACOUSTICS

CONCEPT. At some time in the student's learning, it is important to insure a thorough understanding of the acoustics of the flute. If students can grasp the "how" and "why" of sound production, they will better understand what they are doing, ultimately assisting them in becoming better performers. This section should be incorporated by instructors when the judgement is made that these students are ready, however, educators should not wait too long! A wise approach is to explain the information gradually, and to reinforce it from time to time.

IT'S TIME TO EDUCATE. Often, students obtain a beautiful sound on their instruments without being able to explain how this sound is produced. Right now, the reader may be thinking, sure that may be true but not with my students because every one of them can explain sound production. Well, let's see if there are any brave educators willing to conduct the following experiment.

First, educators should ask one of their top students to teach a lesson, however, the lesson must be taught to the teacher! Educators should pretend they know nothing and ask the student to go through an explanation of how the flute is held, how the flute is assembled, and how a sound is produced. At this point, some educators may be in for the shock of their lives when they find out that although their students can do the things mentioned above, they cannot explain it to others. It is important for these educators to realize that the better the students can explain a concept, the better they will be able to do it themselves thus eliminating many bad habits. These students will also have the potential to become great educators as well as performers. Current as well as future teachers must be able to teach as well as perform. No longer should explanations be given such as "your tone is not right, listen to mine and imitate the sound".

This author has often had college students teaching various aspects of flute playing to master flute classes.

64

This assignment not only helps students evaluate whether
they thoroughly comprehend the techniques they are using
but also whether or not they are playing without any
basic understanding. Many of these students discover
that when they cannot explain a concept correctly to
others, they are not doing it correctly themselves. They
later find out that once they can explain the technique,
they become better performers. If the reader is still
not convinced of the importance of students being able
to explain what they are doing, read on.

FOOD FOR THOUGHT. Recently, there was a flute contest
in which all the contestants were required to play a
certain selection. After listening awhile, it soon became evident that the majority of students consistently
played sharp the notes C and C# when these notes moved
to or came from middle D (see Figure 93).

Figure 93. Understanding of acoustics
makes a better performer.

Upon questioning, none of the students could explain
why this happened. Yet, with a better understanding of
the acoustics of their instrument, many of these students would not only have been able to answer this
question properly, but would have also known what to do
to play the passage more in tune. This is presented at
this point simply to emphasize how important a proper
understanding of tone production is to insure a better
performer. Its answer and similar concepts will be
discussed as this section unfolds.

EDGE TONE CONCEPT. The first point to consider is the
edge tone, or split tone concept. This is the basic
principle from which all sound is produced on the flute.
The edge tone concept can best be described in five
basic steps.

STEP 1. A student blows air across the embouchure hole.

STEP 2. As the air travels across the hole, it is split
into two parts by a sharp edge on the outer edge of the
embouchure hole (see Figure 94).

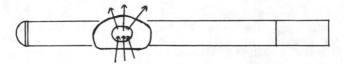

Figure 94. Air travels across embouchure
hole and is split by outer edge.

STEP 3. As the air is split, half the air goes into the
flute and half goes. out (see Figure 95).

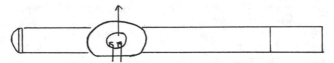

Figure 95. Split air: half goes into flute,
half goes out of flute.

STEP 4. It is the air that goes into the flute that is
set into vibration and produces the sound (see Figure 96).

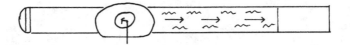

Figure 96. Air entering flute set into
vibration producing sound.

STEP 5. Since the air is split by the edge of the embouchure hole, the resulting sound is thereby referred
to as the split tone or edge tone.

AIR VELOCITY. Through the edge tone concept, the air
enters the flute and a sound is produced. This, in
itself, is not enough to produce a good sound. The
speed by which the air enters the flute also contributes
to the total sound production. Understanding four basic
points should assist the student.

POINT 1. The air which enters the flute will, under
normal conditions, travel up to the first open key. An
example is middle C (see Figure 97).

Figure 97. Air travels to first open key.

POINT 2. As each key is depressed, the air must travel further down the flute (see Figure 98).

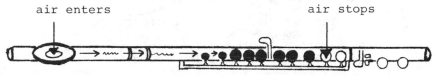

Figure 98. Air travels further down the flute as additional keys are depressed.

POINT 3. Because the velocity of air traveling through the flute has a natural tendency to be greater than the beginning of tone production, it is quite normal for the lower notes to be more difficult to emit. That is the reason low C is difficult to obtain, mainly because the air runs out by the time it gets down the entire length of the tube (see Figure 99).

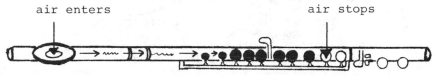

Figure 99. Normal tendency of air to lessen as it travels down the tube of the flute.

POINT 4. Often students become discouraged because low notes on the flute do not come out easily. Once again, if educators would explain why this difficulty occurs, students could then remedy the problem. As mentioned earlier, a thorough understanding makes both a better teacher and performer. Analyzing this situation, it becomes apparent that more air must get down the tube and at a quicker rate of speed so that it gets to the end of the flute faster. To do this, a combination of three things must occur; (1) the lips must be opened wider allowing for more air to come out (see Figure 100), (2) the lower lip should move downward so that more air will enter the flute (see Figure 89), and (3) the student must blow with a little more intensity so that air

will travel down the flute faster. When these points
are understood, instructors may be better able to in-
form their students as to the reason they are having
difficulty playing lower notes, instead of giving them
the typical answer of, "your flute leaks air, have it
repaired".

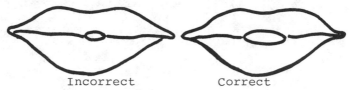

Incorrect   Correct

Figure 100. Wider opening of lips needed
for a good tone in the lower register.

AIR DIRECTION. Once the student understands the importance of the velocity of the air entering the flute, it
is equally important to understand how much air should
enter the flute. This is referred to as air direction
(see Step 10 of this chapter for a more detailed discussion). The following two points should now become
even clearer.

    a.   The lower the sound, the more air into the
        flute. This is achieved by lowering the
        bottom lip which will change the direction
        into a downward direction (see Figure 89).

    b.   The higher the sound, the less air into the
        flute. This is achieved by moving the lower
        lip so that less air will enter the flute (see
        Figure 90).

EMBOUCHURE FLEXIBILITY. It is easy to see how an understanding of the edge tone concept, velocity of air, and
air direction can contribute to a better tone, however,
one other aspect that is crucial is the ability of the
student to have a very flexible embouchure. Without
this, it would be impossible to put air into and out of
the flute with relative ease. The student must have a
flexible embouchure.

PRACTICE MAKES PERFECT. To achieve a flexible embouchure and to insure a thorough understanding of the
above, the following should be practiced daily. Both
the speed and the exercises chosen should depend on the
student's present level. A few exercises to develop a
flexible embouchure are notated below (see Figure 101).
These exercises must be slurred to achieve maximum

reliance on lower lip and to insure the proper concept
of flexibility.

Figure 101. Exercises to develop a
flexible embouchure.

As the students become more advanced, the overtone
series is a wonderful exercise that should be included
in their daily studies. To practice, first have the
student play a low C. Then, without changing the fingering, move the lower lip (jaw) out slightly and the C,
an octave higher, will sound. Maintaining the same
low C fingering and continuing to move the lower lip out
slightly and making the opening of the lips rounder so
that less air will go into the flute, the remaining
notes on the chart shown in Figure 102 will be produced
(see Figure 102). The main point to remember is that
the student should not blow harder to produce the higher
tone, just move the lower lip out and make the opening
of the lips rounder. Figure 102 indicates all the notes
possible on the low C fingering while Figure 103 gives
a few variations that are also helpful in developing a
flexible embouchure (see Figure 103). Remember, the
overtone series does wonders in attaining the lip flexibility needed to become an excellent flutist.

Figure 102. Overtone series.

69

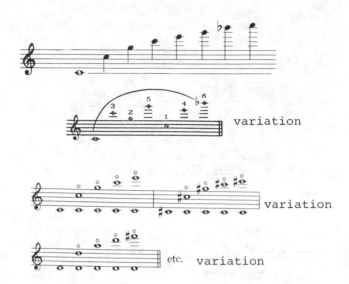

Figure 103. Overtone flexibility
exercises.

The most important points to consider while practicing
the exercises in Figures 101, 102, and 103 are:

a. Don't blow any harder to obtain the higher
tone.

b. Change the direction of the air with a combination of lip opening and lip direction.

c. Let the lips do the work.

BACK TO THE ORIGINAL QUESTION. Going back to the original question at this point will help to determine if any
learning has taken place. Why, then, do the notes C
and C# have a tendency to be played sharp when the melo-
dic line moves to middle D (see Figure 93)? Considering
the following three points should assist the reader in
making the correct response.

a. The air volume is greatest when it first enters
the flute.

b. The air vibrates up to the first open key.

c. The more keys depressed, the further the air
must travel.

Understanding this, the educator must now realize why beginning flutists have a tendency to play sharp the notes C or C$^\#$. Most students, not understanding anything about air velocity, overblow these notes. Understanding the principles readily indicates that the flutist needs very little air to produce this tone mainly because the air has to travel very little down the tube of the flute (see Figure 97). Playing the D which follows involves the air traveling quite a bit further due to the fingering necessary to achieve the pitch. The student must go from practically no keys down to almost all of them depressed, therefore for the middle D, the flute needs more air to produce the proper sound (see Figure 98).

Usually, when a student moves from a C or C$^\#$ to a D, the air traveling through the tube is just right for the D but too much for the C$^\#$ thereby causing the note to play sharp. To remedy this situation, the student must decrease the velocity of the air for the C$^\#$ and increase it for the D. In this manner, the student will play in tune. Further discussion on intonation will take place later, but for now, the reader should realize how vitally important it becomes for the student to not only be able to play the instrument properly, but also to be able to understand and explain exactly the procedure involved.

BREATHING

BREATHING. A major concern for many beginners is proper breathing concepts. Since the flute uses more air than any other wind instrument, it is to the advantage of the performer to know how to breathe properly in order to project the tone or sustain phrases.

Since the production of a flute tone involves splitting the air on the embouchure edge, most flutists utilize only about 25% of the breath. For beginners, it is even less because they have a tendency to open their lips too far and let too much air out. For this reason, many beginners experience periods of dizziness and become tired very quickly. When this occurs, inexperienced students should rest for short periods until the embouchure is better developed and they do not use as much air.

Another cause of dizziness is hyperventilation. Hyperventilation occurs when a student takes in more air than is being let out or when the frequency of breaths is more than normal causing more oxygen in the blood system than is necessary. Once again, until proper concepts

71

are developed, resting for a few minutes should eliminate the dizziness.

In order to eliminate problems such as becoming tired
or dizzy, it is important for students to learn how to
control their breathing as soon as possible. Breathing
is such a natural function that it is often taken for
granted. For instance, as students watch television,
they normally breathe in and out at a regular pace.
While playing or running hard, students will find themselves inhaling and exhaling at a quicker pace, yet it
is still a very regular type of breathing and is quite
natural. As musicians, they find themselves inhaling
quickly and exhaling slowly becoming confused as a conscious effort is made to develop controlled breathing.
Taking in a large amount of air, holding it, and re-
leasing it slowly, is indeed unnatural. It is the educator's job to assist so that this process becomes
natural. Some proven exercises that may help in this
process are discussed below.

WHAT YOU WILL PROBABLY SEE. Ask students to take a very
deep breath and to hold the air as long as possible.
Normally, educators will see the students' shoulders
raise as a breath is taken (see Figure 104).

Shoulders before   Shoulders after
breath.   breath.

Figure 104. Incorrect position of shoulders
after inhalation (front view).

Further inspection will reveal the chest moving up and
out as the breath is taken (see Figure 105).

Chest before breath.   Chest after breath.
Figure 105. Incorrect position of chest (side view).

The educator will also notice the diaphragm area go in as the student inhales (see Figure 106).

diaphragm
area before
breath

diaphragm
area after
breath

Figure 106. Incorrect position of
diaphragm after inhalation (side view).

WHAT YOU SHOULD SEE. As students take a breath, shoulders should not move, but remain in a normal position (see Figure 107).

Shoulders before breath.   Shoulders after breath.

Figure 107. Correct position of
shoulders after inhalation (front view).

Next, the chest fills up with air, however, it does not raise separately but in combination with the diaphragm area which projects out (not in) with a deep breath (see Figure 108).

This concept is often a major problem for students to understand. How is it possible for air to go into an object and the object become smaller? To help students understand, ask them to use a balloon as an example. What happens when air is blown into it? It expands, and so should the diaphragm.

This is a very important concept for the beginner to understand and will be discussed in greater detail later.

73

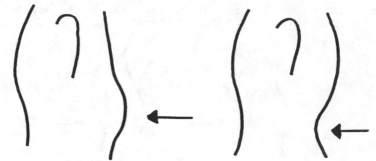

Inhalation diaphragm   Exhalation diaphragm
area   area

Figure 108. Correct position of diaphragm
after inhalation (side view).

BREATHING APPARATUS. Before going any further, a break-
down of the breathing apparatus and its function should
assist students in the development of controlled breathing. By understanding this, students will know why they
must adhere to the instructional techniques described
below in order to achieve proper breath control.
Figure 109 should be studied with great care (see
Figure 109).

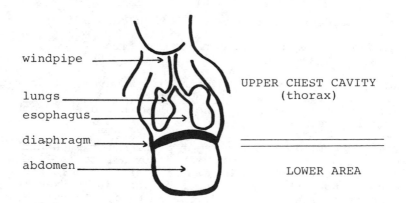

windpipe ——————→   UPPER CHEST CAVITY
                                (thorax)

lungs —————————→
esophagus —————→

diaphragm —————→
                           ————————————————
abdomen ————————→
                              LOWER AREA

Figure 109.   Breathing apparatus.

The breathing apparatus can be divided into two parts,
upper and lower (see Figure 109). The upper section

74

contains the chest cavity (thorax) which contains the
lungs, esophagus, and the windpipe (trachea) (see
Figure 109). The trachea is the pipe in which air
passes in and out of the lungs. To protect this area,
the thorax is surrounded by bones, namely, the spine,
breastbone, and ribs. Between the ribs are a bunch of
small muscles (intercostals) that serve the function
of expanding and contracting the ribs. At the bottom
of the chest cavity is a muscular partition called the
diaphragm (see Figure 109). The diaphragm completely
shuts off the chest cavity from the abdomen or lower
section (stomach area).

During breathing, the first task is to get air into the
system. Normally, air enters the body through the mouth
and then goes down a tube called the windpipe (trachea).
The windpipe extends down the neck and divides into two
tubes each of which goes into the lungs. As the lungs
fill with air they get larger which causes the muscles
between the ribs to move to lift the ribs upward and
outward away from the lungs. This gives the lungs room
to expand. Also, as this happens, the diaphragm muscle
moves down which creates a larger chest area and causes
air to be sucked into the lungs through the windpipe
(see Figure 110).

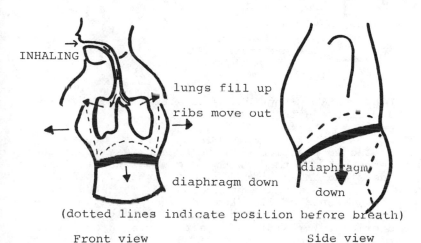

INHALING

lungs fill up

ribs move out

diaphragm down

diaphragm down

(dotted lines indicate position before breath)

Front view   Side view

Figure 110. Front and side view of breathing
apparatus during inhalation

When the air is let out, the muscles between the ribs
move the ribs downward and inward and the diaphragm

moves up forcing the air out. The chest size becomes
smaller, and as it draws closer together, it makes the
lungs smaller further forcing the air out. All of this
is done simultaneously often without any concern because
of its natural process (see Figure 111).

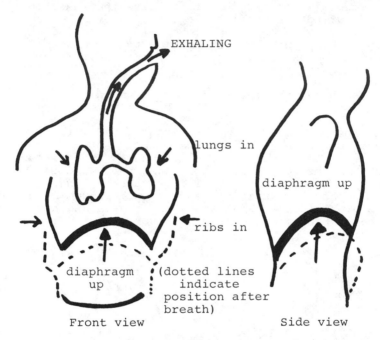

Figure 111. Front and side view of breathing
apparatus during exhalation.

STEPS TO CORRECT BREATHING. During initial stages,
students should practice correct breathing without their
instruments. One method is to have students lie flat on
their backs and in a relaxed manner, inhale, hold the
breath for a few seconds, then exhale. The student, at
this point, should realize that during inhalation, the
diaphragm is moving out, not in. It is helpful if a
heavy dictionary or similar object is placed on the
student's diaphragm. Press down slightly on the object
as the student inhales. This will illustrate how the
diaphragm moves out, and also illustrates the strength
of the diaphragmatic muscles. As students learn to
control diaphragmatic breathing, they should become
aware of how the air must enter the diaphragm area as

well as the chest area. Correct breathing involves the
entire body.

Once this is accomplished, students should practice
breathing standing up. The process is the same. Educators must make certain that the <u>diaphragm comes out
while inhaling</u>! Having students place their hands on
their abdomen will help to demonstrate how the diaphragm
is moving out. If it does, students will then have a
great deal of breath support which, in turn, will increase their endurance. The reserve air in the abdomen
gives the tone life.

GOOD EXERCISES. Since quantity of air is so important
to the flutist, students must look for ways to increase
lung capacity. Developing diaphragmatic breathing
should help. Several exercises are provided to assist
the student. Although there are many different types
of exercises, these have proven successful over the
years.

EXERCISE 1. <u>Crescendo-Decrescendo</u>. For this exercise,
students must stand comfortably with their flutes and
wear some type of belt or rope around their waists.
The belts or ropes must be drawn tightly around the
waist. Next, students should begin to play a scale of
long tones but with a slight variation from the normal
procedure. This time, they should play one note of the
scale at a time beginning very softly and gradually
becoming louder until the note is played fortissimo, or
as loudly as possible. In addition, as the students
play this note, they must gradually move down into a
squat position maintaining a straight back the entire
time. Normally, going into the squat position takes
about ten seconds. Remember, the student starts in a
standing position and plays a single note as softly
as possible. Then, gradually moving into a squat
position, the student should increase the dynamic level
of the tone until it reaches its peak just as the
student completes the squat position.

While in the squat position, the student should continue
to play until all air is emitted. Once this is done,
the student must take a very deep breath. In the squat
position, and with the belts drawn tightly, students
should feel pressure in the abdomen area. If they do
not, they are not breathing correctly.

Once the breath is taken, the process is reversed beginning in the squat position, playing as loudly as
possible, then gradually standing up and gradually

77

getting softer until no air is left. After this is
completed, students should play the next note of the
scale, one note at a time, until the scale is completed.
A diagram for this exercise is provided in Figure 112
(see Figure 112).

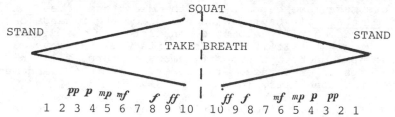

Figure 112. Crescendo-decrescendo exercise.

EXERCISE 2. <u>Arms over chest method</u>. Another helpful
approach to correct faulty breathing habits is to instruct students to hold their arms over their chests in
a V-position grabbing their opposite shoulder with each
hand.   Ask students to push elbows down tightly in the
abdominal area and to take a deep breath. Holding the
shoulders down and avoiding any upward motion of the
shoulders, the students should feel, with their elbows,
the diaphragm area expanding caused by the entering air.
This is what inhaling should be like all the time.

EXERCISE 3. <u>Sleeping method</u>. Since breathing is for
most individuals a natural function, it is helpful to
have students understand how they breathe while in a
sleeping position. To do this, students should lie flat
on their backs and breathe naturally. They will soon
notice how freely the abdomenal area fills up with air.
This occurs on a natural basis each and every night that
the student sleeps. Breathing should occur just as
naturally while sitting up and playing the flute. To
stress this aspect, the author recommends that students,
at times, play long tone scales while lying on their
backs concentrating on proper breathing techniques.

EXERCISE 4. <u>Open mouth method</u>. An often overlooked
reason for students running out of air in the middle of
a passage is because they do not take a large enough
breath.   Sometimes, students inhale through the nose,
the corners of the mouth, or do not open the throat
enough to permit enough air in. This is totally unacceptable and must be corrected at once or students will
never be able to obtain enough air to provide proper
breath support. To provide enough breath, the correct

78

breathing is to open the mouth and inhale as if saying "ooh." This opens the throat enough to permit lots of air in the shortest amount of time, something that is often needed in quick passages.

EXERCISE 5. <u>Marking passages</u>. As students advance, they should become more particular where a breath is taken. Since so much of the air used is wasted on the flute, it is important to breathe at the best possible place. This will help insure maximum control. Students should develop the habit of placing breath marks (') on their music to help eliminate incorrect breathing patterns. This approach can do wonders for students as they begin to learn how to adjust their breathing for short or long phrases. This author suggests that breath marks become standard, beginning with the student's first lesson.

SUMMARY. Controlled breathing is, indeed, a very diffi-cult aspect for the beginner and in many cases, the advanced student, to comprehend. Many students never truly grasp the concept that musicians often do not have the opportunity to breathe at regular intervals. Also, students and performers can go through a lifetime without ever understanding exactly how to breathe and what takes place while inhaling and exhaling.

It is not uncommon for educators to allow students to play for several years without giving serious thought to the concept of controlled breathing. This absence of training can lead to many years of musical frustra-tion. It is the educator's responsibility to avoid this unnecessary dilemma!

CHAPTER IV

DEVELOPING TECHNIQUE

TECHNIQUE I: TONGUING

TONGUING. Tonguing is the first aspect of developing technique that must be completely understood in order to properly execute most musical passages. Over the years, however, this subject has been only briefly introduced in most beginning method books leaving the more detailed explanation up to the instructor. This would be fine if all educators were flutists, but what about those that are not? What do they do?

As a result, most educators find themselves asking such questions as: "When should the elements of tonguing first be taught?" "What are some common problems that beginners encounter?" "Are there different syllables used in tonguing?" and, "When should double or triple tonguing be used?" Questions such as these often confuse instructors to the point where they inadequately prepare their students. The following should provide useful information to make the educator's role a little easier.

QUESTION ONE: WHAT IS TONGUING? Tonguing is often described as the manner in which the tongue is used to articulate tones on wind instruments. The manner of tonguing varies from instrument to instrument and, in each case, it is important to understand the proper procedure of activating the tongue. In the woodwind family, all the instruments except the flute use a single or double reed which the tongue must contact in order to produce a tonguing effect. The flute, however, does not have this concern. For the flutist, the tongue can act as a valve and without a reed to impede its action, can move a lot freer and quicker. As a result, with correct placement of the tongue, a variety of articulations are possible from the harshest staccato to the smoothest legato. Too, because the tongue can move freely, double, triple, and flutter tonguing can be accomplished with relative ease. Since the player can control his tongue better than on other woodwind instruments, clean, precise tonguing is not only desired, but possible to attain.

QUESTION TWO: WHEN SHOULD TONGUING FIRST BE TAUGHT?
Tonguing should be taught after the student has acquired a good steady tone. This varies from individual

81

to individual, however, it usually is taught during the
first lesson in the method book which normally deals
with whole notes. This author usually has the student
repeat the first lesson twice, the first week beginning
each note with the airstream (hoo) to develop the embouchure and tone, then the second week play the same
exercise but begin each note with the tongue. This
approach has proven quite successful over the years.
Tonguing should be introduced as soon as possible <u>before</u>
bad habits develop.

QUESTION THREE: WHAT IS A GOOD METHOD FOR TEACHING
TONGUING? Once the student is ready to tongue, what
method does the instructor use to make certain that proper tonguing techniques are developed? Although there
are a variety of attacks which eventually must be
learned, it is the beginner's concern to develop one
that will lay the framework for the others during latter
stages of playing. One suggestion that has proven
successful for this author is taught in three basic
steps.

STEP 1. The first and probably the most important concept the student must grasp is that THE TONGUE MUST HIT
THE ROOF OF THE MOUTH NEVER THE BACK OF THE TEETH OR
COME OUT BETWEEN THE LIPS. (This author does not recommend the French style of tonguing between the lips.)
The student can best achieve this by pronouncing the
syllable "too" or "tu." By repeating this syllable a
few times, students begin to understand how the tongue
hits the roof of the mouth and get the feel for its
correct position.

STEP 2. Next, ask the student to place the tongue on
the roof of the mouth as if in position to pronounce
the syllable "tu." Keeping it there, have the student
try to emit air from the mouth. This will be impossible
to do because the tongue prevents the air from escaping.
Now, with the air still built up, release the tongue so
the air will come out. Bringing the tongue back up in
the "tu" position once again restricts the air. Repeating this process over and over quickly helps the
student realize how the tongue acts as a valve in controlling the airstream.

STEP 3. Next, transfer this concept to the flute. Have
the student place the tongue in the "tu" position, blow
some air, release the tongue, and a tone will be produced. It's that easy. The student should practice
tonguing several notes in succession to make certain

proper tonguing is achieved (see Figure 113). Now, the student is ready for the printed music.

Figure 113. Transferring tonguing
to printed music.

Remember, as the student progresses, the position of the tongue will vary from note to note, however, this will be dealt with a little later. Right now, the most important concept the student should master is that the tongue must hit the roof of the mouth.

QUESTION FOUR: HOW SHOULD LEGATO AND STACCATO TONGUING BE TAUGHT? Once the fundamental articulation ("tu") is established, students should progress to other types that will further enhance their playing. Two such articulations that should assist in this quest are referred to as staccato and legato style of playing. These two styles occur most frequently at beginning stages and an understanding of the principles behind their production will further assist in the proper development of tonguing at later stages of performance.

Legato is a type of articulation in which the action of the tongue makes a slight interruption of sound between tones. This is accomplished by keeping a steady stream of air flowing and gently interrupting the air by use of the tongue hitting the roof of the mouth. Legato style of playing can be notated several ways (see Figure 114).

Figure 114. Several notations of
legato tonguing.

The notes illustrated in Figure 114 should be tongued, however with a very slight separation. This type of exercise is excellent for the proper development of the tongue because it helps the student eliminate such problems as putting too much space between notes, breathing too often, as is the case with beginning students who breathe after each note, and making certain that the tongue is used to begin each note rather than the use of the breath to begin each note.

Staccato is an articulation in which the tongue is used to stop the tone. Under normal tonguing, the tongue hits the roof of the mouth once for each note ("tu"). Now, the tongue will hit the roof twice, once to begin the tone and once to stop the tone. The syllable used is "tut." Having students repeat the syllable several times will easily demonstrate this principle. Naturally, this type of articulation separates or detaches the notes more than legato playing. It is normally notated as shown in Figure 115 (see Figure 115).

Figure 115. Example of
staccato articulation.

This type of articulation further assists in the proper development of the tongue because it is impossible to achieve without using the tongue. Since beginning students have a tendency to hit the back of their teeth with the tongue, or permit the tongue to protrude between their lips, practicing staccato tonguing will help eliminate these problems. This, however, should not be taught until the student has mastered legato playing.

QUESTION FIVE: WHAT ARE SOME OTHER FACTORS THAT AFFECT TONGUING? As the student becomes more advanced, it becomes increasingly important to learn more about the tonguing process. There are three important points to consider in the further development of a more controlled and positive tonguing action.

POINT 1. Position of the tongue. The tongue should always hit the roof of the mouth but its exact location varies depending on the register of the music. Generally, the lower the note, the further back the tongue strikes,

and the higher the note, the more the tongue moves forward toward the front of the mouth (see Figure 116).

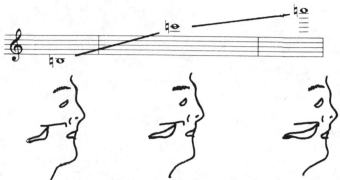

Figure 116. Position of the tongue
according to musical range.

In the extreme upper register, the tongue is usually at
the point where the roof of the mouth meets the teeth,
however, at no time does the tongue hit the back of the
teeth or protrude through the lips. If it does, the
student has moved the tongue too far forward.

POINT 2. Shape of the tongue. The importance of the
shape of the tongue is twofold. First, the syllable
used to begin the tone will determine the type of attack
desired. If a harsh sound is desired, a harsher syllable must be used, and if a softer attack is desired,
a softer syllable must be used. A few of the syllables
used for tonguing are "du", "lu", "tee", "hoo", and
"loo". After pronouncing these a few times, the student will easily recognize which syllables produce a
softer attack or which produce a harsher attack. This
effect occurs as a result of the shape of the tongue
changing as the syllable changes. The chart shown in
Figure 117 should assist the reader (see Figure 117).

SYLLABLE	SHAPE OF TONGUE	ATTACK DESIRED
"hoo"	no tongue used	mildest
"l"	underside	mildest form using tongue
"d"	flat	soft
"tu"	average	normal, used for most playing
"tee"	tip	harsh

Figure 117. Syllable chart for tonguing.

85

Secondly, just as the tongue's position varies from register to register, so does the syllable or shape of the tongue being used. Generally, for the low register, the tongue should be further back on the roof of the mouth and a softer syllable should be used. When the tongue is in this position, air enters the flute quicker and a better sound is produced. Too, since the lower register does not resonate as well as the upper register, using a harsher syllable would make the tonguing more audible than the sound. Often beginners experience this problem because they use "tu" or "tee" in the upper register. Educators who are aware of this tendency can easily correct this concern. Finally, as the notes move up the scale, the tongue moves forward changing its shape from "d" to "tee" in the extreme register.

POINT 3. <u>Loudness</u>. Once again, the shape of the tongue varies but to a lesser degree on volume. Normally, the tongue will be flat while playing soft and more pointed when playing loud.

QUESTION SIX: WHAT IS MULTIPLE TONGUING? Multiple or compound tonguing is used normally in passages that are too difficult to play single tongued. Double and triple are two of the most common types used today by flutists. Both of these are good to employ, however, it must be understood that these are <u>not to be used instead</u> of single tonguing <u>but as a substitute</u> when a passage becomes too difficult to be played under single tongue conditions. Remember, multiple tonguing is not a substitute for laziness but a tool to enhance the performer's ability.

QUESTION SEVEN: WHEN SHOULD MULTIPLE TONGUING BE USED? A question that often arises is when to use double or triple tonguing. Since each student's abilities are different, this author has organized five steps to help determine when to resort to multiple tonguing.

STEP 1. First, get a metronome. Set the metronome on a slow tempo, ♩=52. Now single tongue the passage being practiced at this metronome marking. To demonstrate, Figure 118 will be used (see Figure 118).

STEP 2. If the exercise in Figure 118 is easy to single tongue, move the metronome marking up to the next speed. Once again, single tongue the exercise. If this is still easy, continue to move the metronome up one marking at a time until the point is reached where it is no longer possible to single tongue. For this purpose, let us assume a quarter note will equal 120 (♩=120).

♩ = 52   to   ♩= 120

Figure 118.   Determining use of double tonguing.
First single tongue passage.

STEP 3. Now, move the metronome marking down one tempo
and begin to practice double tonguing. This is important; remember to practice the passage one metronome
marking lower than the point where single tonguing is
no longer possible. Double tonguing must sound comfortable and smooth and going beyond that point may be
acceptable for practice but never for performance. Now
practice the exercise double tonguing (see Figure 119).

♩ = 118

T T K T K T K T   T K T K T K T   T K T K T K

etc.

Figure 119.   Double tonguing exercise.

STEP 4. Once this is accomplished, the students should
gradually increase their double tonguing speed. However, at this point, students should look at the tempo
the composer desires. If it is beneath the quarter
note equals 118 mark (♩=118), then it should be single
tongued, and, if it is ♩=118 or higher, double tonguing should be used.

QUESTION EIGHT: HOW IS DOUBLE TONGUING PRODUCED? Double
tonguing is produced by alternating the front and back
of the tongue in a "T" "K" motion. This approach makes
use of two syllables. The first syllable is initiated
just like single tonguing, however, the second syllable
results when the back of the tongue strikes the palate
to stop the flow of the air. Since many beginning students become confused with terms such as palate, the
author has found that interchanging the word "palate"

with the word "throat" helps the student better visual-
ize and develop the technique.

Since double tonguing provides for a much faster articulation, it is important to develop the technique properly. There are six steps to assist in this process.

STEP 1. As with single tonguing, it is imperative to
begin slowly and gradually work up speed.

STEP 2. Initially, without the flute, have the student
repeat "tu", "ku", or "too-koo" several times. This
will demonstrate the motion of the tongue. The same
procedures should be used in regard to shape and position of the tongue as in single tonguing (see Question
Five). Syllables will change from "doo-goo" to "ti-ki".
These should be developed gradually.

STEP 3. With the flute, begin practice on a note in the
middle register. Make certain that the "goo", "koo", or
"ki" are evenly matched with the first syllable. Sometimes, students emphasize one syllable which makes the
passage sound uneven. Practice Figure 120 using different notes in different registers with their correct
syllables (see Figure 120). Once again, it is important
to use a metronome to insure evenness. Also, caution
must be exercised at this point to make certain that the
second syllable is not voiced. Some beginners keep
their throats too closed and a vocal sound or grunt is
heard.

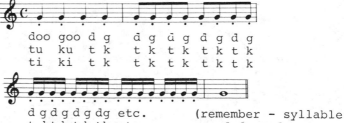

Figure 120. Exercises to develop
different double tonguing syllables.

STEP 4. Some other exercises that may be helpful are
included in Figure 121. They should be practiced in
different keys and different speeds (see Figure 121).

Figure 121.   More double tonguing
exercises.

STEP 5.   Since double tonguing is used for multiples of
two, students often become confused when there are uneven groups of two.   In cases such as these, it is
recommended procedure to have the "tu" or appropriate
syllable fall on the metrically strong pulse. Practice
the rhythmic example provided in Figure 122 using
different notes, scales, and rhythmic patterns (see
Figure 122).

Figure 122.   Double tonguing uneven
groups of two.

STEP 6.   Since it is normal for students to emphasize
the "T" part of double tonguing, the "K", or second
syllable part, is a little weak.   To overcome this, it
is helpful, at times, to practice a passage "goo doo"
or "koo too", reversing the syllables.   Also, practicing
an exercise with just the "goo" or "koo" assists in a
smoother development.   Make certain, however, that the
correct "T-K" or "D-G" approach is used before practice
is finished to make certain that the reverse syllables
become a normal pattern (see Figure 123).

Goo	Doo	Goo	Doo	G D G D G D G D	etc.
Koo	Too	Koo	Doo	K TK T K TK T	etc.
Ki	Ti	Ki	Ti	K TK T K TK T	etc.

Goo	Goo	Goo	Goo	G G GG G G G G	etc.
Koo	Koo	Koo	Koo	K KKK K KK K	etc.
Ki	Ki	Ki	Ki	K KKK K KK K	etc.

Figure 123. Use of weaker double
tonguing syllables.

QUESTION NINE: HOW IS TRIPLE TONGUING PRODUCED? Triple
tonguing is used for passages in groups of three that
are too difficult to play single tongued. It is produced by alternating the front and back of the tongue
within a group of three syllables. Since triple tonguing provides for a faster articulation, it is important
to develop the technique properly. Following the same
steps indicated for proper double tongue development
will assist in this process. There are three ways to
triple tongue. These are:

1. TTK TTK TTK. This is most popular among
   brass players, however, is seldom used by
   flutists.

2. TKT KTK TKT. This is the most practical as
   far as speed is concerned because of the emphasis on a different syllable.

3. TKT TKT TKT. This is the most popular among
   flutists because it gives a very smooth and
   rapid articulation. As with double tonguing,
   the syllable will change from "doo-goo-doo",
   "tu-ku-tu" or "ti-ki-ti" and, likewise,
   practice should be slow and deliberate (see
   Question Five). The exercises in Figure 124
   are intended to give a feel for triple
   tonguing. They should be practiced in
   different speeds, scales, etc. (see Figure 124)

Figure 124. Triple tonguing exercise.

QUESTION TEN: WHAT IS FLUTTER TONGUING? Until recently,
few educators concerned themselves with flutter tonguing,
however, with the current interest in Rock, Latin, and
Twentieth Century composition, it becomes necessary for
the educator to become more familiar with this technique.
"What is flutter tonguing?" "How is it indicated in
music?" and, "How is it done?" are questions most frequently asked. The following should assist the educator
in becoming more knowledgeable in this area of flute
technique.

Flutter tonguing is not an articulation but a special
tonal effect. It first came into use in the symphonic
repertoire of Richard Strauss. There are two ways of
achieving this technique. The most common is to roll
the tongue rapidly against the roof of the mouth as in
rolling the letter R in "brrr". This produces a very
fast tremolo, almost like the sound young children use
to imitate the sound of airplanes or machine guns. With
this type of flutter tonguing, there is no set speed,
but the faster, the better.

Some students may experience difficulty rolling the R.
In fact, there are some that will never be able to do
it. These students may resort to the second method of
flutter tonguing, the gutteral R. This is accomplished
by vibrating the soft palate at the back of the throat.
This is very similar to gargling and often, asking a
student to gargle will quickly give the proper sensation.
This type of flutter tonguing is not as dramatic as
rolling the R because it creates less ripples in the air
stream than the tongue. It is not ideal to rely on this
type of flutter tonguing, however, it certainly helps
those who can do it no other way.

For the advanced student, it is helpful to be accomplished in both methods. As mentioned above, the rolling
R effect is a little harsh. It works fine in the upper
register, however it sometimes interferes with the sound
in the lower register. Often the rolling R becomes
louder than the tone itself. This would be a good time
to use the gutteral sound since it is less abrupt but
still effective. Figure 125 illustrates a good dividing
line, however, it is still an individual matter. When
the two techniques are more refined, choose the technique as desired to give the best control (see Figure
125).

Gutteral   Rolling

Figure 125. Gutteral and rolling R
dividing lines.

There is no set symbol for flutter tonguing, however,
Figure 126 illustrates the most popular notation (see
Figure 126).

flätterzunge, or
flät., or
frullate

Figure 126. Popular flutter tonguing notations.

Finally, flutter tonguing is a good warm up exercise for
the flutist and daily practice before beginning sessions
will relax the lips and keep them more flexible.

QUESTION ELEVEN: WHAT ARE SOME COMMON PROBLEMS FOR
BEGINNERS? Beginners often experience problems that can
be termed common. Since these occur frequently, educators should become aware of these so that they may
correct them immediately before bad habits are formed.
Five of the most common are:

    1. <u>Not tonguing</u>. Often, students do not tongue,
but, instead begin the attack with the breath as if
saying "hoo". Many educators, unless listening closely,
may not notice this. Be observant in this area so that
correct tonguing can be taught at the very beginning.

    2. <u>Tongue between lips</u>. Beginners also have a
tendency to tongue between the lips as if spitting out
a seed. Non-flutist educators may not notice this and,
once again, students develop bad habits. This must be
corrected since this type of tonguing produces a muddy
attack and it is impossible to double or triple tongue
with the tongue protruding between the lips. Some educators use this type of tonguing as an exercise to
strengthen and increase the speed of the tongue of their
more advanced players. This is fine for the advanced
student because it has a definite purpose, however, this

author does not recommend this procedure for the beginning or intermediate player because it may hinder
more than help in the development of proper tonguing
and flute embouchure. Practice with the tongue between
the lips should not be used until proper tonguing concepts are firmly established.

3. <u>Lips or jaw moves</u>. Often, beginners have a
tendency to move their lips or jaws while tonguing.
This is a result of tonguing too heavily. Have students
use a mirror until the problem is corrected.

4. <u>Tongue and fingers</u>. Lack of coordination between the tongue and fingers is a common problem for the
beginner especially when the passage is fast. To correct
this, the student must work on slower speeds concentrating on putting the fingers down exactly as the note is
tongued. Most of the time, students experience this
problem because they try to play a passage fast before
the notes are learned. Since the tongue can move much
faster than the fingers, it makes sense to work out the
passage first.

5. <u>Tonguing variations</u>. Students should practice
with as many variations as possible. This will increase
their ability to control the tongue. A few examples are
given in Figure 127. Practice slowly and gradually increase speed (see Figure 127).

Figure 127. Tonguing variations.

As the student advances, proper tonguing should become
automatic. Becoming aware of the ability to listen to
himself and to constantly ask if the passage sounds the
way the composer intended, should prepare a fine
musical passage. Remember, PRACTICE MAKES PERFECT!

TECHNIQUE II: FINGERINGS

FINGERINGS. Another technique that is extremely important to develop is the use of correct fingerings. With
complications brought on by difficult passages, many
students look for short cuts to eliminate fingering problems. With the use of alternate fingerings, trill
fingerings, harmonics, pianissimo fingerings, etc.,
these short-cut fingerings often become regular fingerings. Since the flute is designed so that each tone
hole is placed where it acoustically produces the best
possible pitch, the beginner should use regular fingerings at all times. The more advanced student may rely
on other fingerings, however, only under careful supervised instruction. This section should assist educators
in becoming more aware of correct fingerings on the
flute.

QUESTION ONE: WHAT NOTE SHOULD BEGINNERS LEARN FIRST?
Educators often realize the importance of correct fingerings for their students, however, frequently fail to
see the importance concerning the initial tone that they
learn. For instance, most method books traditionally
start students with notes that involve the left hand
alone (see Figure 128).

Figure 128. Typical starting tones.

Then, after these tones are learned, the next few
lessons center around other notes involving only the
left hand (see Figure 129).

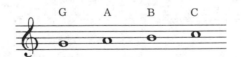

Figure 129. Other typical beginning notes
involving the left hand.

Since the tones in Figure 129 involve only the left hand,
it is this author's opinion that these are not good beginning notes. Often beginners feel insecure in holding

the flute and judge that it may drop while being played.
To compensate for this feeling, and since only the left
hand is needed to play the notes in Figure 129, students
may grab the flute with their right hands in any manner
just as long as they feel secure in holding the instrument.

It is a concern of this author that many instructors
overlook these faulty hand positions judging that they
are only temporary and can be corrected after a few
lessons. Too, many instructors judge that it is more
important to hurry up and play a song than it is to take
the necessary time to correct these mistakes. This type
of reasoning is not correct because it takes twice as
long to correct a bad habit than it does to teach a good
one. What, then, is a good beginning tone? It is this
author's opinion that middle D should be the first note
learned (see Figure 130).

Figure 130. A good beginning tone.

The reasons for this choice are varied. A few are:

   1. Flute feels more secure. Since practically all
the fingers are used for middle D, the flute feels more
secure in the hands of the students, thus they hold the
flute better. As a result, middle D will encourage proper hand position instead of a sloppy one as in the case
of the left hand notes.

   2. Provides for accurate pitch. Normally, beginners are not as pitch conscious as more advanced students. When beginners go home from their lessons, they
often overlook the pitches they are practicing. Sometimes they play higher notes when they should be playing
lower ones (see Figure 131). This is easy to do because
of low notes which have the same fingering as the same
notes an octave higher. Students may practice an entire
week without realizing that they are producing the incorrect pitch. With middle D, however, it is impossible
to produce two different pitches since a different fingering is used for the D an octave lower. Since the
index finger of the left hand is up for middle D (D^2),
it acts as a vent, thus making it impossible for low D
(D^2) to be produced. With this situation, proper pitch

can be developed from the very beginning lessons (see Figure 132).

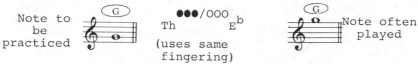

Note to be practiced

Th ●●●/OOO E♭
(uses same fingering)

Note often played

Figure 131. Common pitch problem for beginners. (Notice same fingering).

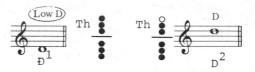

Figure 132. D as the correct beginning note.

3. **Helps establish correct surrounding pitches.** By learning D^2 first, students are better able to establish correct pitches with other notes to be learned. For instance, once the sound of D is established, it becomes much easier to determine if the sound of G^1 is as low as it should be, or, if the student is overblowing it (see Figure 133).

overblowing

D^2 G^1

Figure 133. Using D^2 to establish correct pitches.

Students see that G^1 looks lower and reason that it must sound lower. Thus, by learning middle D first, students may better learn other notes that are often learned incorrectly as beginners.

4. **Initially corrects a commonly misfingered note.** The final reason for learning middle D first is that it is one of the most frequently misfingered notes, even by experienced players who have a tendency to leave the left hand index finger down. Learning this note correctly from the beginning helps to eliminate this common error.

QUESTION TWO: WHAT ARE 'TRICKY FINGERINGS?' Frequently, certain patterns may present fingering problems to the beginning student. Becoming aware of and correcting these problems should increase the student's rate of progress. The following list represents those problems most frequently encountered, explains what students do incorrectly, and discusses how to rectify these problems.

PROBLEM 1. $D^\#/E^b$ key. The $D^\#/E^b$ key is depressed for every note on the flute other than the ones indicated in Figure 134 (see Figure 134). Often, students become careless and do not use this key when they should. Since the fingering system on the flute is built so that each note will sound as acoustically correct as possible, the proper use of this key is essential.

Figure 134. Notes that do not use $D^\#/E^b$ key.

PROBLEM 2. $\underline{C^1 \text{ to } E^1, C^{\#1} \text{ to } E^1}$, etc. Frequently, different combinations of C^1 to E^1 or $C^{\#1}$ to E^1, etc., present difficulties for both beginners and advanced players. The little finger, in this type of combination must be frequently raised or lowered causing a variety of coordination problems. Often, students simply avoid depressing the $D^\#$ (E^b) key to escape this difficulty, sacrificing intonation for ease of playing. This should be avoided. If correct steps are taken during beginning lessons, students should experience no problems later. The exercises notated in Figure 135 should assist in this process. They should be practiced at different speeds depending on the individual student's level of expertise. Make certain the $D^\#$ (E^b) key is down when appropriate (see Figure 135).

PROBLEM 3. $F^\#/(G^b)$. Many beginners experience difficulty with the correct use of the $D^\#$(E^b) key when used in conjunction with $F^{\#1}$, $F^{\#2}$, and $F^{\#3}$ fingerings. Since fingering the $F^\#$'s with the $D^\#$(E^b) key feels awkward, many students avoid depressing the $D^\#$(E^b) key to help ease this uncomfortable feeling. Close supervision should be given to insure proper fingerings (see Figure 136).

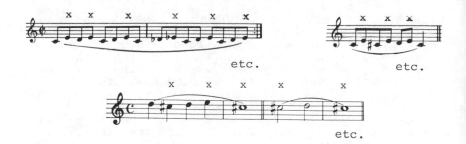

etc.　　　　　　　　　　　　　etc.

etc.

Figure 135. Exercises to develop little finger, right hand (X-keep D♯(E♭) key down).

Practice in all three octaves.

Figure 136. Exercise to develop correct F♯ fingering (make certain D♯(E♭) key is depressed).

PROBLEM 4. <u>High D</u>. D is one of the few notes on the flute that uses three different fingerings. Although similar, it is imperative that each note is fingered correctly to insure proper pitch (see Figure 137).

Figure 137. Three different fingerings for D.

When fingering a middle D (D^2), it is impossible to play a low D (D^1). Also, if a high D (D^3) is fingered, it is still impossible to play a low D (D^1) (see Figure 138). It is possible, however, to finger a low D (D^1) and be able to play a middle D (D^2) or a high D (D^3) (see Figure 139).

Figure 138. It is **impossible** to play a D^1 when fingering D^2 or D^3.

Figure 139. It **is poss-ible** to play a D^2 or D^3 when fingering D^1.

This can be done simply by overblowing or changing the direction of air on the low D (D^1) so that less air enters the flute. This is often referred to as harmonics and when used, gives a softer and flatter sound. Beginners are especially guilty of doing this either because they lack proper training or become sloppy in their technique.

Often beginners make the same mistake with other notes in the third octave, fingering the upper notes according to their lower counterpart and producing the upper partial (see Figure 140). Once again, these will sound both softer and slightly flat. Since the beginner will not enter the area of harmonics for some time, this type of playing is totally unacceptable.

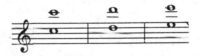

Figure 140. Student playing bottom note often produces upper partial.

PROBLEM 5. <u>Association method</u>. Beginners frequently experience difficulty in remembering the fingerings for the upper notes. A good approach that has consistently worked for this author is described below. First, an assumption will be made that a group of students are having difficulty remembering how to finger high $G(G^3)$. To correct, ask the students to finger a low G^1 or middle $G(G^2)$. Then, simply ask the students to remove their thumb and they will be playing a high $G(G^3)$ (see Figure 141).

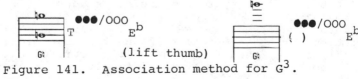

Figure 141. Association method for G^3.

99

Ask students to try another tone. F represents another example (see Figure 142). Once again, ask students to finger low F^1 or middle F (F^2). Now, all students have to remember is to lift up the middle finger of the left hand and the high F (F^3) will sound. Sometimes, instead of thinking of a separate fingering for high F (F^3), which is confusing, students often associate the F^3 fingering with one they already know (F^1 or F^2). This makes the F^3 fingering much easier to learn and retain. This is referred to as the association method.

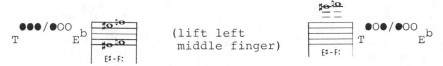

●●●/●OO E^b (lift left middle finger)   ●OO/●OO E^b
T   T

Figure 142. Association method for F^3.

Try this with a few more notes. Finger the lower tone and remove the necessary fingers to obtain the higher tone (see Figure 143).

●●●/OOO● E^b (just change one finger)   ●OO/OOO● E^b
T   T

Figure 143. Association method for $F^{\#3}$).

PROBLEM 6. $\underline{E^b/D^{\#}\text{ fingering}}$. Like D, this note has three separate fingerings (see Figure 144). Great care must be exercised to make certain that each is fingered properly. As with the other notes mentioned above, the association method works well.

                                         $G^{\#}$ (don't forget to add $G^{\#}$)
●●●/●●●   O●●/●●●   ●●●/●●●
T E^b T E^b T E^b

Figure 144. Fingerings for E^b.

High E^b($D^{\#}$) is easy to remember if students are reminded that this note is the only note on the flute that uses all the fingers at the same time. Also, it is a common problem for beginners to keep the left hand index finger up (like E^{b2}) when fingering E^{b3}. Be careful this mistake does not occur! It is difficult to correct!!

PROBLEM 7. c^2 to D^2. This note pattern is often difficult for beginning students because they must move from
using one finger, as in the c^2, to practically all of
the fingers, as in D^2 (see Figure 145). Since this type
of fingering pattern presents numerous coordination problems for beginners, they often resort to the trill
fingering for middle D (D^2) to make it easier (see
Figure 146).

●○○/○○○ $_{E}$b   to   ○●●/●●● $_{T}$

●○○/○○○ $_{E}$b   to   ●○○/○)○○ $_{E}$b
                          (tr1)

Figure 145. c^2 to D^2 presents   Figure 146. D^2 trill
fingering problems.   fingering.

As one can readily see, the trill fingering appears to
make this combination of notes easier to play because
the middle D (D^2) uses less fingers. This fingering,
however, should not be used at this time. Since trill
fingerings are to be used only in very fast passages,
and since it is doubtful beginners will be playing at
rapid speeds, regular fingerings should be used at all
times.

PROBLEM 8. C to D trills. As students progress, one
of the first trills they learn is the C to D trill.
Although a common trill, it is often fingered incorrectly. To finger correctly, c^2 uses the first trill key
while c^3 uses the second trill key. Most students, however, not only use the wrong trill keys, but also the
wrong fingers to play these trills.

For instance, some students move their right hand index
and middle fingers down to play the trill keys. By
doing this, the first trill key will be played with the
right hand index finger while the middle finger of the
right hand plays the second trill key.

This is incorrect! Instead of moving the right hand
index finger and middle finger down, they should be
moved up. By doing this, the <u>first trill</u> key will be
played with the <u>middle finger</u> and the <u>second trill</u>
with the <u>ring finger</u> of the right hand (see Figure 147).

The main reason for using the middle finger for the
first trill key and the ring finger for the second trill
key is to insure freedom for the index finger of the
right hand in the event it must be used to finger a note

101

following the C trill. Observe the samples shown in Figure 148).

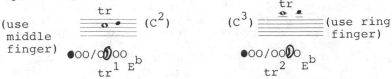

Figure 147. C trill fingerings.

Figure 148. Notes following C trill.

Notice that by using the correct fingers in Figure 148, the index finger of the right hand is free in Example A to play F which follows. Notice, too, how in Example B both the index and middle fingers are free to play the E which follows the trill. Educators must be aware of this to insure fluent technique.

PROBLEM 9. F$^\#$ fingering. Often students play F$^\#$ with the middle finger of the right hand instead of the ring finger. This is a common error, especially among former sax students who switch to flute, because the middle finger is the regular fingering for F$^\#$ on the sax (see Figure 149).

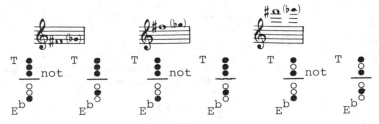

Figure 149. Common F$^\#$ fingering problem.

PROBLEM 10. E to F$^\#$. Often, students use the incorrect fingering for the E^1 to F$^{\#1}$ and E^2 to F$^{\#2}$ pattern resorting to the middle finger to play F$^\#$ (see

102

Figure 150). Once again, regular fingerings must be used except for extremely fast passages or an E to F# trill. Only then should the middle finger be used.

Regular   Trill

Figure 150. Correct F# fingering.

PROBLEM 11. B♭ fingerings. Correct B♭ fingerings are often confusing for both the educator and the student. This confusion results from the fact that there are three B♭ fingerings available for B♭1 and B♭2 (see Figure 151).

Figure 151. The note B♭.

This confusion is further complicated by the fact that in the majority of method books, only one B♭ fingering, referred to as the fork B♭, is explained. The explanation of the bis (lever) B♭ and the thumb B♭ is left to educators to instruct to their pupils when they deem necessary. This would be fine if all educators were flute majors and had prior knowledge of the other B♭'s. This, however, is not always the case and many students progress to the advanced level never realizing that there are two more fingerings for B♭ in addition to the fork B♭ (see Figure 152).

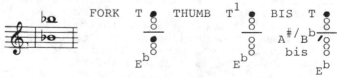

Figure 152. Three B♭ fingerings.

103

To assist in this dilemma, the following general rules are provided:

1. <u>Fork B^b</u> (for B^{b1} and B^{b2}). If there is not a B^b in the key signature, but there are B^b's in the music, use the fork B^b (see Figure 153).

Figure 153. Proper use of the fork B^b.

Also, when there is a B next to a B^b, use the fork B^b even if there is a B^b in the key signature (see Figure 154). This will eliminate the sliding that would take place if the thumb B^b were used.

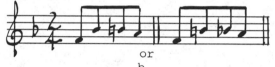

Figure 154. B^b next to B

Finally, use the fork B^b when B^b is next to a tone that uses the index finger of the right hand (see Figure 155). This pattern will work also with the B^b in the key signature.

Figure 155. More uses of fork B^b.

2. <u>Thumb B^b</u>. Use the thumb B^b if B^b is in the key signature. This facilitates the playing of the notes within the composition. Few method books, however, even include its explanation in their lesson materials. This fingering should be introduced <u>early</u> in the student's music career because it will definitely enhance fluent technique (see Figure 156).

104

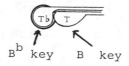

Figure 156. B♭ thumb key.

The B♭ key illustrated in Figure 156 activates a lever
which closes one key on the other side of the flute
(see Figure 157).

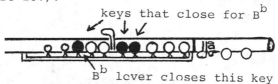

keys that close for B♭

B♭ lever closes this key

Figure 157. Key affected by B♭ lever.

Since this key closes automatically for every other note
except C♯, C and B in the middle register, and B and F♯
in the upper register, the thumb can remain on this key
most of the time without affecting the other tones (see
Figure 158).

Just keep
thumb down
on B♭ key.

Figure 158. Keeping thumb B♭ lever down
throughout musical passage.

Too, with use of the thumb B♭, greater fluency can be
achieved. Attempting the example notated in Figure 159
will illustrate this point. Practice with both thumb B♭
and fork B♭ and see which is easier. Remember to work
for speed.

or

Figure 159. Use of thumb B♭ facilitates technique.

3. <u>Side bis (lever) B^b</u>). The side bis B^b is most
effective in chromatic passages (see Figure 160). It is
played with the index finger of the right hand, almost
at the first knuckle. When using this key, it will be
noticed how light the technique will be and how much
speed can be attained. The side lever B^b is also good
to use in certain trills which are indicated on the
trill chart in Appendix F.

Figure 160. Use of side lever B^b.

SUMMARY. One final word of caution. Since there are so
many different ways of playing B^b, under no circumstance
should a student slide between the B^b and B levers.
Proper thought to each passage and knowledge of the
above should eliminate any confusion and greatly improve
the player's technique.

QUESTION THREE: WHAT ARE ALTERNATE FINGERINGS? WHEN
ARE THEY USED? When a passage moves so quickly that it
becomes impossible to use the correct fingerings and
still maintain the smoothness and evenness required,
alternate fingerings are used. Since beginners seldom
encounter these problems, alternate fingerings should
not be taught until students arrive at a more advanced
stage. The fingering chart provided in the appendix
should be consulted for any note in question. Remember,
however, that alternate fingerings are not regular
fingerings, therefore, they are slightly out of tune.
If alternate fingerings are used as they should be, in
fast passages only, these pitch discrepancies go unnoticed. Educators should introduce these fingerings
as the need arises. A few of the more common alternate
fingerings are given in Figure 161. The regular fingering is always provided first followed by the alternate
fingerings (see Figure 161).

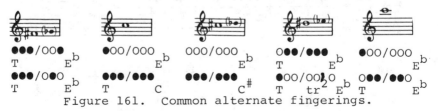

Figure 161. Common alternate fingerings.

106

QUESTION FOUR: WHAT ARE TRILLS? WHEN ARE THEY USED?
Trills are the rapid alteration between two different
tones. At times, these tones move so rapidly that the
use of special fingerings are necessary. These are
called trill fingerings. As in the case of alternate
fingerings, trill fingerings should be used only in fast
passages. Once again, these should be introduced as the
need arises. The list in Figure 162 represents some of
those most frequently used (see Figure 162). A more
complete list is provided in Appendix F.

Figure 162. Frequently used trills.

QUESTION FIVE: WHAT ARE HARMONICS? Harmonics are a
series of notes produced from one basic tone. These are
referred to as the overtone or harmonic series. An example is given in Figure 163 (see Figure 163).

Possible overtones on
low C fingering

Figure 163. Harmonic series.

By fingering low C and properly changing the angle of
airstream that enters the flute, the smaller notes will
be produced without changing the fingering of the low C.
Harmonics are relatively simple for students to produce
and most educators suggest using them in daily practice.
A good exercise to develop lip flexibility is provided
in Figure 164 (see Figure 164). Further discussion
and examples are found in Chapter III (see Figures 101,
102 and 103).

107

etc.

(finger low C throughout excercise)
Figure 164. Harmonic exercise to
develop lip flexibility.

In music, harmonics are notated with a small "o" above
the notes (see Figure 165). They are used basically in
soft passages. To play harmonics, the fingering for
the fundamental tone must be used. Special fingerings
for harmonics on G (first note above the staff) and
above have been included in Appendix F. These are considered standard today, but should be used by advanced
students only. A detailed explanation of harmonics can
be found in Appendix A.

Figure 165. Example of notated
harmonic tone.

TECHNIQUE III: INTONATION

INTONATION. Intonation and good tone quality go hand
in hand, yet it is surprising how many players can go
through a lifetime without understanding the mechanics
behind good intonation. Although playing in tune is
ultimately the responsibility of the performer, the educator must also take the initiative to teach students
not only how to recognize when pitches are out of tune,
but also how to bring them back in tune. The following
steps are provided to assist in making the task of
developing good intonation easier.

STEP 1. WARM UP THE INSTRUMENT. Before students can
begin improving their intonation, they must make certain

108

that their instruments are warmed up. The temperature
of the flute has a direct bearing on its intonation.
Usually, for instance, when students begin to play,
their intonation is not very good. This occurs as a
result of the flute being too cold. A general rule concerning the temperature of the instrument is, the colder
the flute, the flatter the sound; the warmer the flute,
the sharper the sound. Since the speed of sound increases with a rise in temperature, when a student warms
up the flute the pitch becomes higher and the flute
plays better in tune. So before making any other adjustments, warm up the flute. This can easily be done
by playing a few long tone exercises or scales. Some
flutists find that fingering low C (low B if applicable)
and blowing a quick burst of air directly into the embouchure hole, adequately warms up the instrument.

This author prefers to use the 'quick burst' method <u>only</u>
when it become necessary to keep the flute warmed up between numbers, during a live performance. It is apparent that the method of warming up is an individual
matter, just remember to <u>do it</u>!

STEP 2. <u>CHECK PLACEMENT OF THE CORK</u>. The next step toward better intonation is to make sure that the cork in
the headjoint is in the correct position. The importance of this cannot be overstated since correct posi-
tioning is essential for correct intonation in all
registers. It is good procedure to have the first chair
flutist check the cork placement of the rest of the
flute section at least once a week. This can be done by
inserting the cleaning rod into the headjoint until it
touches the cork. The line etched on the cleaning rod
should be exactly in the center of the embouchure hole.
An important point to remember is that the cork is not
a tuning device. It is placed there to close the end
of the pipe. Its location is critical to the overall
intonation of the instrument, and once set, must not be
moved.

STEP 3. <u>TUNE A SINGLE NOTE</u>. Once the flute is warmed
up and the cork is in the correct position, it becomes
possible to make a basic pitch adjustment. This is
accomplished by tuning to a single note, usually A or B♭.
If the note is not in tune, adjustments can be made by
pulling the headjoint out if the note is sharp, or, by
pushing in if the pitch is flat. If the instrument is
still playing flat once the headjoint is pushed in all
the way, or if the headjoint is pulled out more than a
quarter of an inch, the fault lies in the embouchure
and not the instrument itself.

STEP 4. <u>BECOME AWARE OF NOTES THAT PRESENT PITCH PRO-
BLEMS AND HOW TO CORRECT THEM</u>. Because of the construction of the flute, there are a series of notes which re-
quire special adjustment while being played (see Figure 166). Students, in order to improve their intonation, should be aware of these problem tones and understand how to correct them.

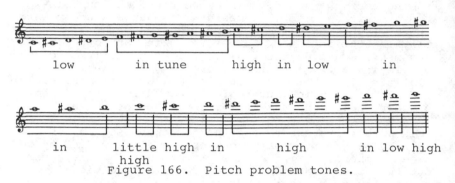

Figure 166. Pitch problem tones.

From observing Figure 166, it is apparent that the
general tendency of these notes is to be sharper in the
upper register and flatter in the lower range. Too, it
can be seen that the extent of variation in the pitch
of the tones is directly proportional to the length of
the tubing used to produce the tone. For instance, if
the middle C or C# notated in Figure 167 were played mf,
they would, in all probability, be in tune since the air
needed to produce these tones does not have to travel
far (see Figure 167). Most students, not realizing this,
would probably use too much air, overblow the pitch,
causing the tone to be sharp. Thus, the tones notated
in Figure 167 have a natural tendency to be sharp.

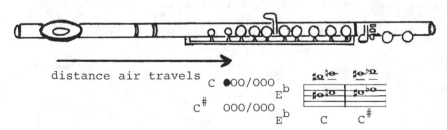

Figure 167. Notes have a general tendency to
be played sharp when the air does not have to
travel far down the instrument.

110

On the other hand, if low C or C# were played at the
same dynamic level, mf, these tones would probably be
flat since the air must now travel the entire length of
the instrument (see Figure 168). Students, often not
realizing this, do not use enough air causing the tone
to be flat. Thus, the lower register has a natural
tendency to be played flat.

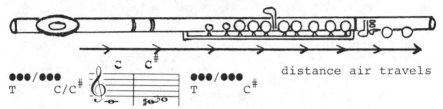

distance air travels

Figure 168. Notes have a general tendency to
be played flat when the air must travel
further down the instrument.

Recognizing and understanding why these tones have a
tendency to be played out of tune, students will find
it much easier to control them and play them in tune.
To assist in this process, six basic points will be
treated. Improving intonation can involve the use of
any of these aspects singularly or by using a combination, depending on each individual case. (For further
information, it is suggested to read Appendix A and to
reread the section on intonation found in Chapter III.)

POINT 1. Changing velocity of air. Changing the
velocity of the air entering the flute directly affects
the pitch of the tone. A general rule is, the greater
the velocity of air entering the flute, the sharper the
pitch; the less velocity of air entering the flute, the
flatter the pitch. Understanding this concept, the
player will better be able to adjust some of the problem notes shown in Figure 166 (see Figure 166). For
instance, if the C^2 and $C^{\#2}$ notated in Figure 167 have
a natural tendency to be played sharp, decreasing the
amount of air entering the flute will lower the pitch
helping these notes to play more in tune (see Figure
167). The principle of increasing the velocity of air
for the low C^1 and $C^{\#1}$ notated in Figure 168 will help
raise the pitch to its normal intonation (see Figure 168).

POINT 2. Dynamics. Another important area that directly affects intonation is how loud or soft a note is to
be played. Referred to as dynamics, its proper use can
greatly improve intonation problems. This, however, is

111

not often the case. Normally, without any change of
embouchure, etc., a note being played loud (ff) will
have a tendency to be sharp, while the same note played
soft (pp) has a tendency to be played flat. Using loud
or soft as the only criteria for keeping notes in tune
is absurd, yet, many students attempt this method. These
students end up performing passages so poorly that they
totally ruin the interpretation of the piece being
played.

Consider the musical passage notated in Figure 169 (see
Figure 169). The dynamic marking is forte throughout.
If students attempt to adjust to the natural tendencies
of each note (to be sharp or flat) by using volume alone,
the passage immediately loses its musical style and
beauty.

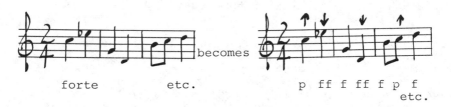

forte   etc.   p ff f ff f p f
                                                                 etc.

Figure 169. Improper use of dynamics
to control intonation problems.

Therefore, the use of dynamics <u>alone</u> is not enough to
control intonation problems. Proper use of dynamics
involves the proper use of the speed of air entering
the flute. Dynamics and velocity are directly related.
Students must better understand this relationship and
how it can improve their intonation. First, with an
increase in the velocity of air entering the flute, the
tone not only becomes louder but also sharper in pitch.
Therefore, in playing a crescendo, the pitch will get
sharper and sharper unless the embouchure compensates
(see Figure 170).

cresc.

Figure 170. The pitch becomes sharper
during a crescendo unless the embouchure
compensates.

112

To correct this tendency of the tones becoming sharper during the crescendo, the player must change the angle of the air so that it is directed more and more into the embouchure hole. This will keep the pitch down and correct the problems mentioned above.

On the other hand, with a diminuendo, the pitch will become flatter and flatter (see Figure 171).

decresc. or

dim..

Figure 171. The pitch becomes flatter during a diminuendo unless the embouchure compensates.

To compensate for this, as the velocity of the air diminishes and the tone becomes softer, the direction of the air is gradually raised forward or up by moving the lower lip out putting less air into the instrument.

Although moving the lower jaw in or out is considered the best approach in correcting faulty intonation, some performers resort to simply lowering or lifting the head to put more or less air into the instrument. This may work fine if the passage is very slow allowing for the movement of the head, however, if the passage is quicker, the lower jaw or lip method should be employed. Some performers even resort to rolling the flute in and out with the hands to adjust the amount of air entering the flute. This author does not recommend this procedure because it creates sloppy hand position and the movement is too jerky to be very effective.

Though the above techniques may be used singularly or in combination, the fact remains that this delicate technique of developing a good relationship between velocity and direction of air must be consciously developed. Simply stated, it just doesn't happen overnight.

POINT 3. Practice with a straight tone. Often students use vibrato as a disguise for intonation problems. This is a common fault and should be avoided. Practicing with a straight tone is the best procedure when working on intonation because it is easier to hear pitch discrepancies and to adjust until correct. Remember, vibrato is to enhance, not to disguise.

POINT 4. <u>Place markings above notes</u>. Placing symbols
above tones to indicate whether a note has a natural
tendency of being sharp or flat helps the student become more conscious of these tones and to adjust accordingly. These marks can be eliminated when this recognition becomes automatic. This author likes to place
an arrow either up or down above the notes in question
(see Figure 172).

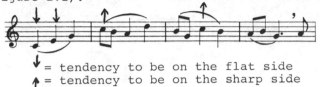

↓ = tendency to be on the flat side
↑ = tendency to be on the sharp side

Figure 172. Developing an awareness of
intonation by the use of symbols.

POINT 5. <u>Correct fingerings</u>. Using correct fingerings
is a must for correct intonation. A few of the common
problems are listed in Figure 173 (see Figure 173).
Educators must be conscious of this and correct immediately. (For more information, reread Technique II of
this chapter.)

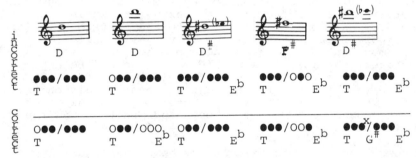

Figure 173. Common fingering problems.

POINT 6. <u>Faulty instrument</u>. It is impossible to
achieve proper intonation if the instrument is not in
good mechanical condition. The flute should be checked
on occasion to make certain that the pads don't leak
and that the keys are not too high above the tone hole.
These two factors which affect the intonation of a note
are frequently overlooked by educators while attempting
to improve a student's technique.

POINT 7. <u>Other factors</u>. Practicing scales, octaves,
and chords are all helpful in improving intonation. It

114

is often good to practice in unison with another flutist to determine where pitch discrepancies occur. This normally encourages the players to listen to each other and become extremely conscious of intonation problems.

SUMMARY. It becomes apparent that educators should no longer have their students tuned to one note. There are simply too many variables to correct intonation. Tuning to a single note, such as an A or B^b, simply means that only one note is in tune. What about all the others? By understanding the preceding information, it becomes apparent that it is best to tune to several tones at various dynamic levels (see Figure 174). By tuning to similar notes as those notated in Figure 174, students must think of all the variables involved in good intonation as well as adjust to achieve the proper pitch.

Figure 174. Tuning to several notes at various dynamic markings.

This approach keeps the student conscious of the technique of good intonation which will ultimately produce a finer performer.

TECHNIQUE IV: VIBRATO

VIBRATO. Another important technique to develop is vibrato. Vibrato is essential in flute playing because it not only provides for a better tonal quality, but it also creates intensity and gives direction to musical line.

The subject of when and how to teach vibrato often arises among music educators. It is sad to admit, however, that many students are never taught vibrato, and even worse, those that have been taught have received incorrect training. Common statements such as, "my instructor told me vibrato cannot be taught but that it must be a part of you," or, "the best way to learn vibrato is to listen to others and then imitate them," demonstrates the need for a better understanding of vibrato. The following pages are devoted to that task.

QUESTION ONE: WHEN SHOULD VIBRATO BE TAUGHT? The best
time to teach vibrato is when a student can adequately
sustain a steady tone within all three registers of the
flute. This, however, does not imply the complete range
because many students do not acquire that technique until they become more advanced. Since vibrato should be
taught prior to that, many bad habits may develop if
educators wait too long. The range indicated in Figure 175 is considered adequate (see Figure 175).

Figure 175. Sustaining a steady tone within
this register indicates readiness for vibrato.

Often, students who wait too long to learn vibrato, develop a "nanny goat" sound. This is a constant, un-
ceasing, repetitive pulsation that causes audiences to
question whether they are listening to flute players
performing, or if they are in a field of hungry,
bleating sheep! This type of vibrato is totally unacceptable and is usually a result of the students'
inability to produce a steady tone. Since a prerequi-
site to vibrato is the development of a clean, pure,
steady tone, it would be futile to instruct before that
aspect is acquired. If students cannot control this
element, vibrato would only hinder, not help the sound.

QUESTION TWO: WHAT IS VIBRATO? To understand exactly
what vibrato is, one must first think of it as a supple-
ment to an already existing sound. Vibrato does not
create sound, but instead, enhances it.

To produce vibrato, therefore, it is first necessary to
create a steady tone. This tone will result as the
performer releases a steady stream of air into the
instrument (see Figure 176).

— — — — —

Figure 176. First step to producing
vibrato is a steady tone.

Once this steady sound is accomplished, vibrato can be
produced by varying the speed of the airstream in regular pulsations so that the pitch produced will no longer

116

be steady. These pulsations are usually four to six
per second.

As vibrato is produced, the pitch first becomes louder
and consequently a little sharper in pitch. This is
caused by an increase in the velocity of the airstream.
Next the pitch becomes a little flatter as a result of
a decrease in the velocity of the airstream entering
the flute. One complete cycle in the airstream is
called a pulsation. Combining these pulsations creates
vibrato (see Figure 177).

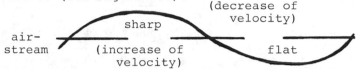

Figure 177. One pulsation of vibrato.

QUESTION THREE: HOW IS VIBRATO PRODUCED? Once the students understand what vibrato is, they must learn how it
is produced. What exactly does a person have to do
physically to create pulsations necessary to produce
vibrato? Understanding this concept will aid the instructor in the teaching of vibrato and dispel any
further myths that it cannot be taught.

Vibrato is produced by using the throat constrictor
muscles and the diaphragmatic muscles. These may be
used separately or in combination. Diaphragmatic vibrato is produced by increasing or decreasing the wind
pressure by a controlled motion of the diaphragm and
surrounding muscles. To accomplish this, the diaphragmatic muscles must first push in, forcing more air
into the instrument. This sudden increase of airstream
produces the sharp portion of the vibrato cycle.

Next, a slight hesitation occurs before the next push.
It is during this hesitation that less air enters the
flute producing a decrease in the velocity of air entering the flute. This decrease causes the flat portion of
the pulsation cycle. Controlling this technique provides for a beautiful tone, however, this author judges
that this type of vibrato has its limits because the
diaphragm itself is not capable of moving more than one
time per second. Generally, an ideal vibrato is four
pulsations per second.

Throat vibrato involves the constrictor muscles which
control the amount of air entering the instrument.
These muscles contract and expand permitting just enough

air in and out to complete the cycle necessary for vibrato. This technique is similar to that of a vocalist
except the syllable used is silent. To open and close
the constrictor muscles, it is best to use the syllable
"hah." When this syllable is sounded, it pushes forward more air to create the upward motion of the pulsation cycle, and when the throat is released, the downward motion of the cycle results. When students practice this syllable with the instrument, it may, at times,
sound like a dog panting. This sound is correct. This
type of vibrato is used mostly because of its ease and
its ability to produce a faster pulsation.

To produce the ideal vibrato, the students should be
able to interact the two when necessary. If the musical
passages call for a slower vibrato, students should begin each pulsation with the "hah" and, at the same time,
push in with the diaphragm giving the tone maximum
support (see Figure 178).

three pulsations

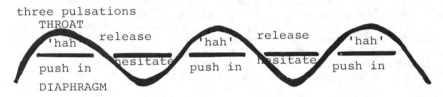

Figure 178.   Interaction of throat
and diaphragm vibrato.

If the musical passage calls for a quicker vibrato, begin the cycle with "hah" and at the same time push in
with the diaphragm. This time, however, the pulsations
continue with the throat "hah" while the diaphragm elim-
inates the hesitation aspect as it continues pushing in
to support the tone (see Figure 179).

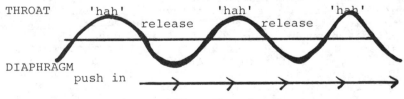

Figure 179.   Throat vibrato.

QUESTION FOUR: HOW IS VIBRATO TAUGHT? To determine if
students are ready to learn vibrato, ask them to play

118

the scales notated in Figure 180 (see Figure 180).

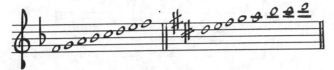

Figure 180. Scales to determine if students
are ready to study vibrato.

The scales in Figure 180 should be played as long tones
without any specific meter. Students should be able to
play each note from beginning to end without any deviation from a steady pitch. There should be no quiver or
irregular pulsation of any kind. If this occurs, correct before going any further (see Figure 181).

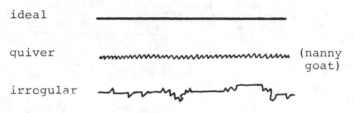

Figure 181. Strive for straight tone.

If a steady tone is attainable, the students should begin the study of vibrato. Six basic steps are provided
to assist in the actual teaching and playing of vibrato.

STEP 1. Without using the tongue, begin a half note by
using the syllable "hah." At the same time, accent the
"hah" by pushing in with the diaphragm (see Figure 182).

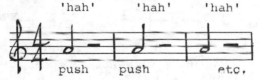

Figure 182. First step to vibrato.

STEP 2. After half notes are developed, change the
rhythm to quarter notes. Once again, begin the attack
with the throat at the same time pushing in with the
diaphragm. Using quarter notes helps to develop a
little quicker pulsation (see Figure 183).

119

Figure 183. Quarter notes, the
second step to vibrato.

STEP 3. The next step is to eliminate the rests. This
will develop an even quicker pulsation. At this point,
it is still not necessary to connect each note but to
continue separating them with the "hah" effect (see
Figure 184).

Figure 184. Third step to vibrato,
eliminate rests.

STEP 4. Now, begin to connect the pulsations attempting
to have no space between the notes. This is done by
following the same procedure of starting the tone with
the throat, continuing to push in with the diaphragm,
and using the throat to produce the syllable "hah."
The main difference, however, is that the airstream must
not be interrupted. The notes sound almost like a
breath accent (see Figure 185).

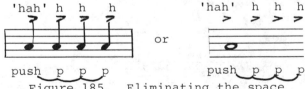

Figure 185. Eliminating the space
between the notes.

STEP 5. Once this is controlled, change the beginning
of the attack for each note by using the tongue and then
continuing with the vibrato technique (see Figure 186).

tah h h h   tah h h h
push p p p   push p p p

Figure 186. Begin each note with the
tongue and continue using vibrato.

120

STEP 6. Continue to practice the above, changing notes so that the students will become accustomed to playing vibrato in different registers.

QUESTION FIVE: HOW IS A CONTROLLED VIBRATO DEVELOPED? After the basics are learned, students must acquire better control over vibrato. There are numerous exercises that will assist the student, yet, no matter which exercise is used, it may appear more mechanical than necessary. To insure maximum use of vibrato at later stages, however, these mechanical steps are most necessary. One such exercise is provided that will demonstrate how, through a mechanical approach, controlled vibrato can develop.

STEP 1. Practice the exercise notated in Figure 187 using four vibrations per beat. Begin at a slow speed and gradually increase the tempo markings when necessary. Also, it is a good idea to change scales from time to time to break up the monotony of daily practice. This author includes above each student's exercise a brief sketch of what occurs on each beat of music so that students will better understand what they are trying to attain (see Figure 187).

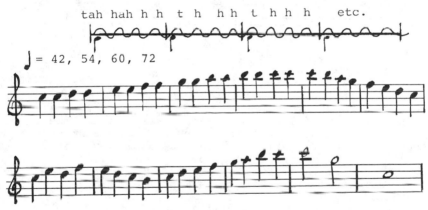

Figure 187. Practice exercise for controlled vibrato.

STEP 2. After step one is attained, it is advisable to play the same exercises using different pulsations per beat. Once again, this may appear mechanical, but through this endeavor comes the flexibility needed later (see Figure 188).

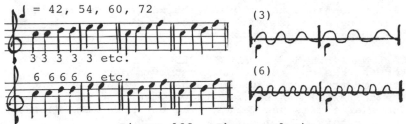

Figure 188. Three and six
pulsations per beat.

STEP 3. Next, to develop even better control, alternate the pulsations and continue to vary the tempo
markings (see Figure 189).

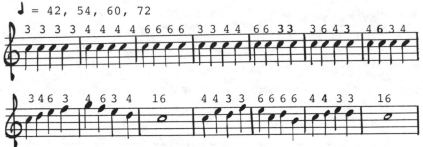

Figure 189. Alternating pulsations.

STEP 4. At this point, it is important to introduce
vibrato into actual music. Once again, the mechanical
approach is necessary. The pulsations at the slower
tempo will sound more exaggerated, however, as the tempo
becomes faster, the pulsations should become smoother
and narrower, yet still remain clearly audible. It is
also good procedure to practice the exercises notated
in Figure 190 in different octaves depending on the
individual's capabilities (see Figure 190).

Figure 190. Incorporate vibrato into a musical example.

QUESTION SIX: WHAT ARE THE "ABC'S" OF VIBRATO? It was
stated earlier that vibrato not only contributes to
better tonal color, but also creates intensity and gives
direction to musical line. These "ABC's" of vibrato are
the heart to the player's tone. They are crucial to the
overall interpretation of a musical composition. A
better understanding of each should demonstrate the use-
fulness of vibrato in music.

"A." First, without vibrato, the tone has a tendency to
be boring. The only effect possible is to play either
loud or soft. A straight tone may also sound nasal,
easily played out of tune, or sound weak without any
other support. Vibrato improves this situation by giving more center to the tone. This helps the tone to
resonate more which contributes to better tonal color.

"B." Intensity is the next aspect which is created by
adding to a crescendo a vibrato that grows with speed
and agitation (see Figure 191).

crescendo (cresc.)

Figure 191. Using vibrato to create intensity.

Reversing the process can give the opposite effect and
bring about a feeling of relaxation (see Figure 192).

decrescendo (decresc.)

Figure 192. Using vibrato to create
a relaxed feeling.

"C." Finally, vibrato gives direction to a musical
line. If used correctly, vibrato can give the listener
a feeling of knowing exactly where a series of notes
are within a musical phrase. If the phrase is ending,
normally the vibrato decreases, and at the peak of a
phrase, vibrato may be at its greatest. Too, there may
be times when it is not necessary to use vibrato and a
different effect is created. All of these assist in the
interpretation of the piece and through vibrato, the
breath of life is given to the selection.

SUMMARY. Vibrato provides for a more interesting and varied tone. It must be developed with patience and care. To avoid the risk of developing bad habits, vibrato must be taught, not imitated. Ultimately, the success of vibrato control depends upon the musical sensitivity and imagination of the individual. This chapter should provide for a proper beginning in that quest.

CHAPTER V

INSTRUMENT CARE

Instruments are beautiful to see and hear, but
they are also delicate. Students, not realizing this,
often damage their instruments by improper handling.
Just think of the times flute players have placed their
instruments across a music stand, or clarinet players
have left their instruments unattended, resting on the
bell. In both cases, the instruments could have easily
fallen causing considerable damage. Experienced educators must sadly admit that instances such as these do
occur. An example, once experienced by this author,
further illustrates the thoughtlessness of students
concerning instrument care.

It was the end of the school year and the
band was practicing for commencement exercises.
The rehearsal was being held outdoors. Also,
it was that time of year when many of the flute
players, who doubled as majorettes during
marching season, were thinking of the upcoming
summer practices where they would have to re-
tire their flutes for the "good old baton."

After an hour of practicing, the band was
given a ten minute break. Upon resuming rehearsal, it was noticed that six flute players
had disappeared. After patiently waiting for
another ten minutes without any sign of the
girls, a search was conducted. They were soon
located on the other side of the school building practicing vertical tosses with, of all
things, their flutes!

Is there any doubt in the reader's mind that there
should be more emphasis placed on instrument care? If
not, let's begin.

DAILY FLUTE CARE

DAILY FLUTE CARE. There are several daily steps to be
followed to insure proper flute care. These are listed
below.

STEP 1. CLEANING THE INSIDE OF THE FLUTE. Just as the
mouth should be cleaned after each meal, so should the
flute be swabbed after each use. This is necessary because a clean bore is not only more sanitary, but produces a clearer tone. Also, moisture that is left in

the flute may cause the pads to swell resulting in poor seating of pads. To clean the inside of the flute, one must use a cleaning rod (see Figure 193).

Figure 193. Flute cleaning rod.

Since the cleaning rod comes with the flute, it must be an important part of the instrument. Right? It would appear so, yet a recent study conducted by the author revealed that out of 200 public school flute cases checked, an overwhelming 70% of the cases did not have a cleaning rod! Since it is impossible to clean the instrument without a cleaning rod, educators must make certain that there is one in every flute case. To use the cleaning rod, put a soft, lintless cloth, similar to a handkerchief, through the opening located at the end of the rod. The procedure is similar to threading the eye of a needle (see Figure 194).

Figure 194. Placing a cloth through the eye of the cleaning rod.

It is important to cover the entire end of the swab from the tip down to the end so the inside of the flute will not become scratched (see Figure 195).

Figure 195. Cover the tip of the cleaning rod.

Now, clean each section separately holding the end of
the cloth firmly with the fingers. Place the cleaning
rod into the headjoint (see Figure 196), the body (see
Figure 197), and the foot joint (see Figure 198). Use
a twisting motion for best results. Notice that the
middle joint must be cleaned from both ends since the
cleaning rod is not long enough to clean it in one
motion (see Figure 197).

Figure 196.   Figure 197. Clean   Figure 198.
Clean headjoint   body from both ends   Clean foot joint.

STEP 2. CLEANING THE OUTSIDE OF THE FLUTE. Regardless
of which material a flute is made, the outside should
be wiped off after each use. Many students fail to
take the time to do this not realizing that the potential accumulation of dirt and perspiration may gather
in the rods and keys causing the action to slow down.
Also, the luster may become dull if not wiped off after
each use. Flutes made of sterling silver have a tendency to become a little dull or tarnished. This is
normal for flutes of this type, however, wiping off
after each use diminishes the chance of this happening.
This situation is very similar to mother's fine silver-
ware that must be wiped off before each use to obtain a
better shine. Sterling silver flutes are no exception.

A flute can tarnish simply from being out in the air as
a result of pollution in the air. Also, the amount of
acid in the player's system may contribute to the degree the flute tarnishes. It should be pointed out, however, that the performance of the flute is in no way
affected by the degree of tarnish. The following procedure for cleaning the surface of the flute is quite

127

simple. Its daily use will not only limit the tarnishing but also keep the flute in better playing condition.

a. The flute should be wiped off before putting it back in its case.

b. Using a soft cloth dampened with warm water is best for the beginner. (This author likes to use rubbing alcohol when possible because it evaporates quickly, thus, the flute is not exposed to unnecessary moisture that may get on the pads.)

c. Students should wipe only the areas where the hands and fingers touch. Try to stay away from pads, etc. Don't forget to wipe the embouchure plate.

d. Often, dust accumulates between the keys and springs. Students should remove dust with a Q-tip or a small paint brush.

CAUTION. Caution students to stay away from the pads while cleaning the flute. If the pads get excessively wet, they will not function properly. Also, avoid cleaning the flute with silver polish!! This material contains abrasives, and although the instrument may look pretty when cleaned, it may not play as well as it did before it was cleaned. This is a result of the silver polish accidentally getting on the pads which causes the skins to break and the pads to leak air. Too, silver polish may work its way between the rods and keys causing the mechanism to become sluggish, and bind. Remember, avoid silver polish!!

STEP 3. CLEANING SOCKETS AND TENONS. Sockets and tenons usually work best when both surfaces which come in contact with each other are kept clean. Wiping off on occasion should keep dirt from building up which may eventually make it difficult to assemble the instrument. To clean, simply use a soft cloth and wipe clean. If dirt accumulates making it difficult to get the joints together, dampen the cloth with rubbing alcohol or water. Be sure to clean both the outside of the flute joint tenons plus the area they enter the sockets. A good procedure is to first clean the headjoint tenon (see Figure 199), then the socket and tenon of the middle joint (see Figure 200), followed by the socket of the

128

foot joint (see Figure 201). One last word, most students assume that the flute just fits together and oft-
en overlook this important area of instrument care.
Knowledgeable educators will not allow this to happen.

Figure 199.   Figure 200. Middle   Figure 201. Foot
Headjoint tenon.   joint socket and   joint socket.
                      tenon.

CAUTION. Some educators advocate the use of oil or
grease to help the joints go together more easily. This
author advises against this procedure. These materials
have a tendency to collect dirt and grit particles in
the air which act as an abrasive. In time, this abrasive may wear down the joints to the point where they
will fit together too easily. If this occurs, the problem may then be one of keeping the flute together instead of putting it together! Another factor, too, is
that grease and oil have a tendency to dampen the vibrations of the flute often causing a rough sound.

One final point, if the flute does fit together too
easily, don't panic. With a special tool called a
reamer, a competent repairman can expand the joints
quite easily.

REGULAR MAINTENANCE

REGULAR MAINTENANCE. There are several areas that
should be checked on a regular basis to insure a properly conditioned flute. These are listed, as follows.

STEP 1. STICKY PADS. On occasion, pads may stick on
the flute. Humidity is the main cause, thus, sticky
pads are more a problem in summer than in winter months.
If pads do stick, cigarette paper or lens paper should
help. To remedy, take the paper and place it between
the key sticking. Then, depress the key and gently
pull out. If you do not have any paper with you, a
dollar bill will do in an emergency. The dollar bill
contains oil from humans handling it, and when used in
this manner, it leaves some oil on the pads which helps
eliminate the stickiness.

Some educators recommend talcum powder to remedy the
problem. Just take a little powder, place on a piece
of paper and slide between the sticky key. Depress the
key gently and pull the paper out. Enough powder should
stick on the pad to remedy the problem. (This author
recommends that this method be supervised and used only
in an emergency situation. If not, students may get too
much powder on the pad causing it to deteriorate to the
point where it has to be replaced.)

One last suggestion is to dip a pipestem cleaner into
alcohol and lightly brush across the surface of the pad.
Do not apply too much since it may remove some of the
natural oil on the pads causing them to dry up and split.
(This author recommends applying a light coat of key oil
to any pad that the alcohol may have dried out. Once
again, use a pipe cleaner.)

Finally, if the pad still sticks after attempting the
above, it is best to replace it.

STEP 2. CHECK CORK PLACEMENT. The cork placement of
the headjoint should be checked frequently. Often flute
sections in bands and orchestras do not play in tune.
Not understanding the reason why, both conductors and
students become frustrated in their attempts to rectify
the problem. This problem could be nothing more than a
faulty cork position in one of the player's headjoint.
To help eliminate this problem, it is recommended to
have the first chair flutist check the headjoints of
the other flutists once a week to insure that the corks
do not slip out of placement. The best method to do
this is to take the cleaning rod and find the line near
its end (see Figure 202).

Figure 202. Cleaning rod measuring line.

This mark has a specific purpose. Place the rod into the headjoint until it cannot go any further. The line on the rod should appear directly in the center of the embouchure hole (see Figure 203).

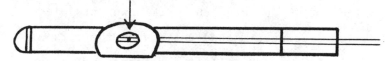

Figure 203.   Notch appears in center.

If the line is too far in or out, the cork should be moved accordingly (see Figure 204).

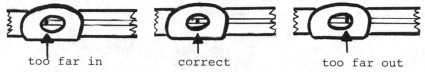

too far in   correct   too far out

Figure 204.   Correct and incorrect
position of headjoint cork.

Students should not move the cork unless trained because the cork can be damaged if it is forced to move. A competent music director or repairman can do this in a few minutes. For those desiring to learn the proper procedure, four basic steps are provided.

  a. Take the crown or nut off (see Figure 205).

Figure 205.   Taking the crown off the headjoint.

  b. If the cork is too far down, push it back
      with the cleaning rod until properly
      lined up (see Figure 206).

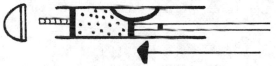

Figure 206.   Pushing the cork into place.

  c. If the cork is too far up, push the cork down
      with the cleaning rod from the crown side
      (see Figure 207).

131

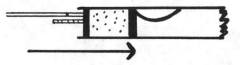

Figure 207. Pushing the cork down into place.

    d. An alternate method for moving the cork is
        to unscrew the crown just enough to push
        it down or to pull it out depending on the
        direction desired (see Figure 208).

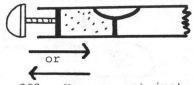

Figure 208. Unscrew nut just enough
to push in or pull out cork.

The procedure is simple but care should be taken not to
force the cork because it might wear down to the point
where the cork will slip, possibly during performance.

CAUTION. Never tamper with the cork with the idea of
tuning. The crown assembly is not intended as a tuning
device. The cork must be exactly 17mm from the center
of the embouchure hole. The line on the cleaning rod
gives this exact measurement. The precise location of
the cork is critical to the tuning and intonation of
the entire range of the flute. The upper notes especially will be badly affected by a faulty positioned
cork.

STEP 3. OIL KEYS AT PROPER PIVOT POINTS. Often keys
may appear sluggish giving very slow key action. In
some cases, keys that are depressed may not come back
up. Much of this can be eliminated by oiling the pivot
points on the flute. It is the same principle as
driving a car without oil; eventually, big trouble!
Proper oiling is important (see Figure 209).

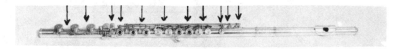

Figure 209. Oil keys at proper pivot points.

132

Oiling, however, should be done not more than once or twice a year, and then only if necessary. A competent repairman or music director should do this for the student unless the student has been properly trained. If a student is careless, he may use too much oil, it may drip onto the pads, and the pads may become ruined. Only a tiny drop is necessary. Investing in an oil pen is helpful because usually only a drop falls down the pen eliminating the worry of using too much. If it is not possible to invest in an oil pen, a drop of oil on the end of a pin or toothpick will do. Please use woodwind oil and not mother's cooking oil!

STEP 4. WASH HEADJOINT. Occasionally wash headjoint with warm water and a mild soap. Before washing, the cork must first be removed. Unless a student has been properly trained, this should not be attempted. There are three steps in removing the cork. They are:

    a. Remove the crown (see Figure 210).

Figure 210. Remove the crown
from the headjoint.

    b. Push the cork assembly toward the bottom
        end of the headjoint with the cleaning
        rod (see Figure 211).

Figure 211. Push cork down flute.

It is necessary to push the cork down toward the tenon because the headjoint is slightly conical, thus the cork would not fit through the other end. Unaware of this, many students have ruined the cork by forcing it incorrectly out of the headjoint (see Figure 212).

133

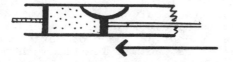

Figure 212. Never push cork out of
flute toward crown.

c.   To replace the cork, reverse the process
     making certain the cork is in the proper
     position before replacing the crown.
     Use the line on the end of the cleaning
     rod to determine the cork's exact position.

STEP 5. AVOID GRASPING THE KEYS. Avoid grasping the
keys whenever possible (see Chapter II). Many students
are careless in this area and damage an otherwise perfect flute.

STEP 6. CLEAN THE EMBOUCHURE HOLE. This is an often
overlooked, yet extremely important, point in flute
care. Since the flute is dependent on a clean split air
column (see Chapter III), the cleaner the edge, the
better the chance of producing a pure sound. To clean,
use a Q-tip and dip in rubbing alcohol. Gently rub
around and along the embouchure hole in an up and down
motion, almost like brushing teeth (see Figure 213).

Figure 213.   Clean edge of embouchure hole.

STEP 7. CHECK FLUTE CASE. Periodically, a check should
be made to see if the flute is being placed in the case
properly (see Figure 214). Students who are in a hurry
often throw the flute into the case with the keys in the
wrong direction and damage the flute (see Figure 215).

Flute 214. Correct placement of flute in case.

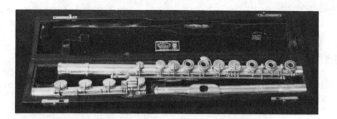

Figure 215. Incorrect placement of
flute in case in which G# key can
easily be bent.

Occasionally, educators should conduct an unannounced
check to see what else is kept in the flute case other
than the flute. Don't be surprised to find music,
combs, pencils, chapstick, and other incidentals. Does
it sound silly? Wait and see!

STEP 8. ADJUSTING SCREWS. The flute has several adjusting screws. These are located on the keys closed by
the second, fourth, fifth, and sixth fingers (see
Figure 216).

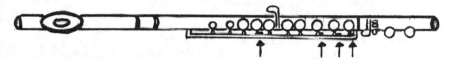

Figure 216. Adjusting screws.

These screws help adjust the opening and closing of keys
that coordinate with the key being depressed. An example would be the F key. When it is closed, two other
keys close. If they do not close properly, a fuzzy tone
will result. By using the adjusting screw on the F key,
these two other keys can be adjusted properly (see
Figure 217).

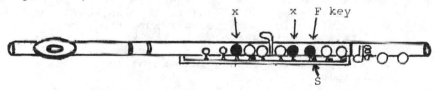

Figure 217. Pressing the F key also depresses
keys marked X. Adjusting screw marked S will
raise and lower keys marked X until they all
open or close simultaneously.

STEP 9. CHECK RODS AND KEYS. With the beginning flutist, bent rods and keys occur at an alarming rate.
Check occasionally because bent rods and keys prevent
a clear tone and even technique, something the beginner
should have. Students should not attempt to fix these
since proper repair involves taking the keys and rods
off the flute. This should be done by a competent repairman who has the proper tools.

STEP 10. LEAKY PADS. If a student who is developing a
good tone suddenly produces an airy or fuzzy tone,
suspect a leaky pad. The following methods may be helpful in locating the leak.

    a.   Take the flute apart. Close the bottom end
       of the middle joint (body) with a cork. If
       a cork is unavailable, put the end of the
       middle joint directly on the knee and press
       down gently. This will seal the tube similar
       to the cork. Now close all the tone holes
       with the fingers. Blow air through the open
       end of the joint without pressing down hard
       on the keys (use normal pressure). If there
       is a leak, air will be heard escaping from
       the faulty pad.

    b.   If possible, purchase a leak light. They
       are inexpensive and an excellent way of
       locating a leak. To operate, simply plug
       the end of the joint as stated above, insert
       the light into the flute, press down the
       keys, and look to see if there is any light
       shining through the pads and the tone holes.
       If light is noticed, it could be a faulty
       pad.

    c.   Be extra careful with the $G^{\#}$, $D^{\#}$, and trill
       keys. Often, air escaping does not mean a
       bad pad, but instead, a weak spring. To
       check, plug end of joint, depress keys, and
       blow a quick burst of air into the tube.
       If the springs are weak, the keys will come
       up a little causing air to escape. If this
       happens, the spring must be strengthened or
       replaced.

Once a leaky pad is located, it will have to be either
reseated or replaced. If the skin on the pad is worn
or damaged, replace. If it isn't, reseat by using
feeler paper. This is done by moving the paper in a
circular motion under the key. While depressing the

key, make certain that the pressure felt on the feeler paper remains constant. If, while moving the paper around, there is suddenly less pressure, move the pad until the pressure becomes uniform.

STEP 11. GENERAL OVERHAUL. In order to prolong the life of the flute and to insure ease of playing, a general overhaul is recommended every few years depending on the use of the flute. This must be done by a competent repairman and is well worth the money.

STEP 12. USE FLUTE CASE. When not playing the flute, either hold it or put it in its case.

SUMMARY. Too many students think that there is no need to take care of their instruments, especially if it is not an expensive model. Regardless of the price, however, it is imperative that students take good care of their instruments no matter what the care costs. Taking proper steps to insure a mechanically sound instrument will make the task of playing the flute much easier.

Remember, a flutist can play only as good as his instrument will allow.

CHAPTER VI

THE FLUTE FAMILY

It has become increasingly necessary, in recent
years, for musicians to learn to play instruments other
than that of their primary interest. Flute players are
no exception often doubling on the saxophone, clarinet,
oboe, or bassoon. Before this occurs, however, flute
students should become more familiar with the other
members of the flute family, namely, the piccolo, E^b
soprano flute, the alto flute in G, and the bass flute
in C.

The information provided in this section is not
only for the interested student, but also to show educators the limitless opportunities of incorporating
these flutes into their music programs.

PICCOLO

PICCOLO. Ah, the piccolo, that tiny instrument that
causes so many frustrating moments for both the performer and the director. To exemplify this point, consider
a question frequently asked, "Why is the piccolo often
isolated and treated like the black sheep of its family?"
Evidence may indicate that this may be the general
feeling since the United States is the only country
that does not use the term "little flute" in regard to
the piccolo. For instance, the French use "petite
flute," the Germans "kleine flote," the Spanish "flautin"
and the Italians "ottavino." All of these terms mean
"little flute" while the word piccolo simply means
small. Too, consider for a moment how all the other
members of the flute family have the word flute after
their names while the piccolo does not. There is the
soprano flute, the concert flute, the alto flute, the
bass flute, and then there is the piccolo!

Additional questions like: "Why is it difficult to
play the piccolo in tune?"; "When should students begin
to play the piccolo?"; "How many piccolos should there
be in an instrumental organization?" or, "Is piccolo
playing the same as flute playing?", indicate the need
for a better understanding of the instrument. Since
the piccolo is one of the most popular members of the
flute family, several areas will be explored to assist
in making it a more understood instrument.

I. WHEN SHOULD A STUDENT BEGIN PLAYING PICCOLO? This author recalls giving a lesson to a student who arrived with a piccolo instead of a flute. Upon questioning, the student indicated that the music store was out of flutes to rent, therefore, the piccolo was suggested as a replacement. The reasoning was that the piccolo was similar to the flute and that good piccolo players were in great demand. The student's parents agreed, and purchased the piccolo.

This was definitely a mistake. The piccolo is not for the beginner, but should be considered as a double once the student becomes accomplished on the C flute. The only way a student can become accomplished on the piccolo is if the flute embouchure is first well developed. The piccolo should be for the best student, not the worst.

II. IF NOT FOR THE BEGINNER, WHO SHOULD PLAY THE PICCOLO? If piccolos are not for beginners, who are they for and when should students begin playing them? Understanding four basic points should be helpful in determining these factors.

POINT 1. Select a child with thin lips. This can be done by a quick visual glance among those being considered. Remember, the thinner the lips, the better it will be for the student to adjust to the smaller opening on the piccolo.

POINT 2. Select a child with good intonation. Choose a child who can perform well in all aspects of flute performance, however, pay particular attention to one that has good intonation. Testing them to see if they can distinguish whether a note is being played sharp or flat is helpful.

POINT 3. Select a child with small fingers. Because of its miniature size, choosing a child with small fingers is helpful in achieving proper hand position on the piccolo.

POINT 4. Select a child on the advanced level of performance. Choosing the worst student will not help at all. That is the reason most knowledgeable educators choose their second or third best players to play the piccolo. Normally, the first chair flutist does not double on the piccolo because of the demands of playing all the solo flute parts.

One final word concerning the use of the piccolo. Often there may be a flute student who has a spongy, "gold fish" embouchure. This type of embouchure is too loose to produce the proper sound. To assist in correcting this, it is advisable to have the student play the piccolo for a short time. Since the piccolo uses a firmer embouchure than the flute, it provides the necessary muscle tone that the student may be lacking. Try it for a short time and return to the flute. Chances are that the flute embouchure will be greatly improved.

III. HOW MANY PICCOLOS SHOULD BE IN AN ORGANIZATION? Some music directors judge that it is best to have as many piccolos as possible in their organization. Although this may be the case for the marching season where projection is important, caution should be exercised during concert season. An overabundance could be extremely detrimental.

Since the piccolo plays higher than any other wind instrument, it deals in extremely high frequencies. These frequencies are capable of projecting out and above the other wind instruments. In many cases, one piccolo can be heard projecting above the entire brass section. As the notes ascend on the piccolo, the tonal target becomes smaller and smaller and the frequencies accumulate in ratios that are unbelievably high. Because of this, the slightest alteration in pitch will cause the pulsations produced by the sound to chatter. This chattering will go unnoticed if the piccolos are being played in tune. Since perfect intonation is quite difficult for most students to achieve, this chattering becomes extremely noticeable, especially in the upper register. At times, it can affect the intonation of the entire ensemble.

The above is not intended to frighten the music educator but to make him aware of a common problem. It is possible to eliminate the chattering effect by using only one piccolo or adding on in ratios of odd numbers. For instance, with three piccolos the sounds counteract with each other and proper intonation is easier to achieve. With four piccolos, the chattering continues because of even pulsations. With five, the sounds counteract with each other again. How many piccolos to use is an individual matter, however, remembering that there should be no groups of even numbers will help. The rest is up to the performer.

141

IV. WHAT ARE SOME POSITIVE ASPECTS THAT WILL ENCOURAGE PICCOLO PLAYING? Piccolo playing can be a rewarding experience, however, many students avoid playing one because they hear so many negative comments. As a result, educators sometimes discourage instead of encourage. There are four points that have proven successful in presenting the positive side to piccolo playing. These may be helpful in the recruitment of some fine students. They are:

POINT 1. The C flute is an extremely popular instrument. To achieve any type of recognition, one must play extremely well. Students who play equally as well on the piccolo will find themselves more in demand than other correspondingly good flutists who only play the flute.

POINT 2. The piccolo is much smaller in size than the flute, therefore, it is possible to play fast passages with relative ease.

POINT 3. The piccolo offers the chance to be heard, while flutes sometimes get lost in the sound of the entire ensemble.

POINT 4. Because the piccolo uses less air than the flute, it is possible to play many passages with correct breathing which often present problems for the flutist.

V. WHAT SPECIFICATIONS ARE IMPORTANT FOR THE PROPER SELECTION OF THE PICCOLO? The basic specifications for the purchase of a piccolo are the same as with the C flute (see Chapter I) except for the type of material used. It is possible to buy both a wood and silver piccolo. Knowing which is best should help the educator properly guide students who are interested in purchasing a piccolo.

Ideally, the wood piccolo is the best. The wood adds resistance which helps the sound more nearly match the quality of the flute than does the silver piccolo. The experienced player may not have many difficulties with the wood instrument, however, the occasional player may encounter numerous obstacles. For instance, the wood piccolo does not have a lip plate to rest the lip, thus, the lower lip may slip off the headjoint. Another problem encountered with the wood piccolo is trying to produce a tone that will not drop in pitch. This problem can be overcome if the proper amount of air enters the piccolo. This technique

can be acquired with proper training. Also, there is
the additional worry of the wood piccolo cracking because a careless student may drop it or subject the
instrument to extreme temperature changes.

Considering these problems, it is the author's
opinion that the wood piccolo is best for the professional player. For practical reasons, the silver
piccolo is considered ideal for most public school
situations. The silver piccolo is not only easier to
play but, also, students do not have the added worry
of the instrument cracking. Most public schools should
invest in the silver piccolo.

Bore size is also important when selecting a piccolo. It is possible for the bore on the piccolo to be
either cylindrical or conical. With the conical bore,
the body of the piccolo tapers very gradually. That of
the cylindrical bore does not. The conical bore is
recommended for the professional musician who must use
a variety of tone, dynamics and color. The only problem is that the piccolo with the conical bore is more
difficult to manage; however, the professional musician
should be able to meet the challenge. The piccolo with
the cylindrical bore is more for the casual player. It
plays easier, especially in the upper register. It is
also less expensive and one that most public schools
can afford.

VI. WHAT STEPS ARE IMPORTANT FOR PROPER PICCOLO CARE?
The care of the piccolo is similar to that of the
other flutes. The wood piccolo deserves some special
attention in regard to temperature change. First, the
student must never warm up a wood piccolo by blowing
a sudden burst of air through it. This will cause a
different rate of expansion between the interior and
the exterior diameter which may occur at such uneven
rates that the instrument will crack. The best procedure is to allow the piccolo to warm up to room temperature before playing. The metal piccolo, however, can
be warmed up the same way as the other flutes, simply
by depressing the keys and blowing gently into the
instrument.

Most piccolo players keep the instrument inside
their jacket pocket to keep it from getting cold when
it is not in use. This helps it to remain warmed up
and is more likely to be in tune the next time it is
to be used.

VII. DO STUDENTS EXPERIENCE ANY PROBLEMS DUE TO THE
PICCOLO'S SMALLER SIZE? The piccolo is considered the
smallest member of the flute family. Although its
basic approach is identical to the concert C flute, its
greatly reduced size presents several problems. First,
students find that it is much more difficult to hold
the instrument and often judge that they will drop it.
To correct this, an adjustment of the hand position
must be made to compensate for the miniature key work.
Other problems directly related to its size are a
result of the very small opening of the hole in the
embouchure plate, the faster speed of air necessary to
produce a tone, and numerous intonation problems. This
will be discussed below, however, for now, it is important to recognize that playing the piccolo is no different than playing the flute except that everything must
be reduced to its proper proportion.

VIII. WHAT IS THE PLAYING RANGE OF THE PICCOLO? The
range of the piccolo is the same as it is for other
members of the flute family except that it descends
only to a low D (^{1}) not having the necessary keys to produce a low C (C^1) or C$^\#$ ($C^{\#1}$). Too, except for the
professional musician, high B (B^3) and C (C^4) are
usually avoided because of the great demand necessary
to produce them. The occasional player, in an effort
to produce these tones, may pinch too much and ruin an
otherwise perfect embouchure. The piccolo is in the
key of C and sounds an octave higher than written (see
Figure 218).

written   sounds   range of
actual sounds

Figure 218. The piccolo range.

The piccolo is often considered an extension of the
regular flute with the low register of the piccolo
matching the second octave of the flute and continuing
on to the concert flute's high C in a homogenous scale
(see Figure 219). Since the piccolo can perform quite
easily in this range, it is often used to support the
upper register of the C flute which is, at times,
difficult for the student flutist to play properly.

144

(sounds the same)

PICCOLO   FLUTE

Figure 219. The piccolo as an
extension to the C flute.

Although rarely found in today's ensembles, educators
may encounter a Dᵇ piccolo. This instrument looks
exactly like a C piccolo except that it begins on a Dᵇ
and sounds a half step lower than the C piccolo. Years
ago, when Dᵇ piccolos were popular, there was a separate
part written in Dᵇ. Today, however, very few publishers
include a Dᵇ part in their scores. If a Dᵇ piccolo is
encountered in an organization, simply rewrite the part
up a half step.

IX. WHAT ARE THE BASIC PRINCIPLES OF TONE PRODUCTION?
The procedure for producing a tone on the piccolo is
the same as it is for the C flute except everything is
done to a smaller degree. Four basic points should be
considered in the production of a good piccolo tone.
They are:

POINT 1. Adjust lower lip on embouchure plate. The
hole on the embouchure plate is greatly reduced in size.
To compensate for this, placing the embouchure plate a
little higher on the lower lip than is done with the
flute assists in directing the air at the proper angle
necessary to produce a good tone.

POINT 2. Properly direct air across embouchure hole.
Proper direction of air is crucial on the piccolo because of the very small size of the opening. If this
aspect is not developed carefully, much air will be
wasted. Great care must be exercised to insure a
smaller stream of air enters the piccolo at the right
angle. The slightest deviation can tremendously affect
the intonation.

POINT 3. Adjust aperture properly. The piccolo needs
more breath pressure and quicker air speed than the
flute. Yet, because of the smaller opening, it actually
uses less air. A student must be able to adapt this
principle in order for the tone to resonate more.

145

POINT 4. <u>Use a firmer embouchure</u>. The embouchure must be firmer on the piccolo than on the flute. This assists in making the opening in the player's lips smaller and to use more intense, yet, less air.

X. WHAT ARE SOME COMMON INTONATION PROBLEMS STUDENTS MAY EXPERIENCE? Although manufacturers have tried to minimize the difficulties involved in piccolo performance, there are still a few common problems that the educator should be aware of. Some of these problems occur because of student carelessness while others are a result of a compromised piccolo.

The compromise occurs with the embouchure hole. The existing hole presently perfected by manufacturers is what is considered normal for most players, however, if the piccolo were built according to proper specifications, the embouchure hole would be one half of the existing one. This hole would, indeed, be small and it would be highly improbable that there would be anyone with small enough lips to produce a tone. To remedy this, manufacturers compromised by building an embouchure hole that is smaller than the flute yet bigger than necessary for the piccolo.

The knowledgeable educator should help his students become more aware of this compromise, point out the intonation problems this may present, and help them in making the situation work. Understanding five basic concepts should assist in this goal.

PROBLEM 1. The tones notated in Figure 220 have a tendency to be sharp or flat (see Figure 220). To correct, follow the recommendations outlined in Chapter IV.

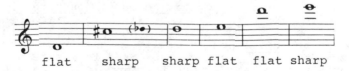

    flat   sharp   sharp flat   flat sharp

Figure 220. Problem tones
for the piccolo.

PROBLEM 2. The high B^b (B^{b3}) and C (C^4) are extremely difficult to obtain on the piccolo (see Figure 221). It is not recommended that students begin practicing these notes until on the advanced level. In an effort to obtain these notes, many students resort to pinching which may ruin their embouchure. Although a firm

146

embouchure is necessary to play the piccolo, there should be no overabundance of tightness. The best procedure is to raise the little finger of the right hand which will help produce the tone more easily.

B♭   C

Figure 221. Raising little finger of the right hand will assist in production of B^3 and C^4.

PROBLEM 3. The high B (B^3) is difficult for many students to produce (see Figure 222). Substituting the D trill key for the D# key should assist in producing a better sound.

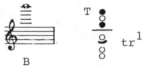

B   tr[1]

Figure 222. Substituting the D trill key for the D# key on B^3 helps it to play easier.

PROBLEM 4. High G# ($G^{\#3}$) is often difficult to obtain because of the extra wind pressure required to produce the tone. Using the fingering notated in Figure 223 should help (see Figure 223). Also, using the correct fingering but omitting the D# key helps the note speak a little easier (see Figure 224).

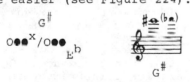

G#

O●●ˣ/O●● E♭   G#

Figure 223. Substitute fingering for $G^{\#3}$ on the piccolo.

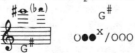

G#

G#   O●●ˣ/OOO

Figure 224. Omitting the D# key assists in producing the $G^{\#3}$ on the piccolo.

147

PROBLEM 5. Since the ultimate goal of a fine piccolo
player is to achieve good intonation, it is very helpful
to mark a line on the instrument so that it will be
aligned at exactly the same spot each time it is assembled. By doing this, performers insure themselves of
working with the same angle every day which is quite
helpful in achieving proper tone production.

SUMMARY.

     One final word of advice concerning the piccolo. It
takes a special kind of student to play one, someone
that is not intimidated. To state it in simple terms,
there just isn't any place to hide.

     Too, since there are few piccolo methods presently
available, the best procedure is to adapt the flute
literature already available. One book that should
help the flutist who is beginning to play the piccolo
is Learning the Piccolo by Clement Baron (Schirmer).
This book deals with the problems of playing the
piccolo in relation to the flute. It is excellent and
worth investigation.

     Yes, the piccolo can be a rewarding experience.
Just remember that the piccolo is an extension of the
flute and if treated as such, will be easy and fun to
play. The piccolo is, indeed, a "little flute."

E^b SOPRANO FLUTE

E^b SOPRANO FLUTE. The E^b soprano flute is an interesting instrument because it combines the blend of both
the piccolo and regular flute qualities. Because of
restricted budgets, few schools own one, however, this
author judges that it would be worth investigating the
possibility of purchasing an E^b soprano flute.

I. WHAT SIZE IS THE E^b SOPRANO FLUTE? The E^b soprano
flute is four inches shorter than the concert C flute.
As a result, this is an excellent instrument for the
young flutist who desires to play a C flute but is not
able to because of short arms. The E^b flute offers the
opportunity for the child to begin lessons at an early
age and then to switch to a C flute when physically
able. Too, because of its smaller size, the E^b flute
is easier to handle and uses less air to produce a
sound. These are also advantages to the young flutist.

II. WHAT IS THE PLAYING RANGE OF THE E^b SOPRANO FLUTE?
The E^b soprano flute has the same three octave range as
the other flutes and sounds a minor third higher than
the printed tone (see Figure 225). The soprano flute
is capable of producing a pure sound in any register and
provides a solid blend between the piccolo and flute.

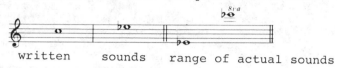

written   sounds   range of actual sounds

Figure 225. E^b soprano flute range.

III. WHAT ARE THE BASIC PRINCIPLES OF TONE PRODUCTION?
The basic principle of tone production is very similar
to the concert C flute. The most important difference
is the embouchure opening being slightly smaller thus
using less air to produce a tone. See Chapter III to
review proper sound production.

IV. WHAT ARE SOME USES FOR THE E^b SOPRANO FLUTE? Many
ensembles are incorporating the soprano flute in their
flute sections as a third flute. Because of this, the
soprano is often referred to as the "terz" flute,
meaning third or interval of a third. This flute provides added support and provides new and interesting
tonal qualities when used within the E^b sections of a
band or orchestra. Many public school bands use the
soprano flute as a substitute in the absence of the E^b
clarinet.

These reasons, in addition to its use as a substitute
instrument for a beginner who is too small to play the
concert flute, makes the soprano flute worth investigating by present day music educators.

CONCERT C FLUTE

CONCERT C FLUTE. The concert C flute is the most popular member of the flute family. Its versatility
warrants its use from Bach to Rock. Too, the concert C
flute has the largest repertoire available and one that
meets the needs of any interest. Since the concert C
flute is dealt with almost exclusively in this manual,
it needs no further attention at this point.

149

ALTO FLUTE. Another member of the flute family is the
alto flute. Relatively new in popularity among musicians, this flute has been in existence since late 1800.
It's inventor, Theobald Boehm, recognized as the father
of the modern day flute, considered it his favorite
instrument (see Appendix B). Apparently, others did
not share Boehm's enthusiasm because few musicians in-
vested in one. Even today, except for top-rated professional musicians, few people own one. Public schools
are no exception as very few educators incorporate the
alto flute in their programs. Originally, unavailabil-
ity was blamed for not owning one, however, today many
companies not only manufacture alto flutes, but make
several different models. Later, the excuse for not
owning one was the fact that very little music· was ever
written for the alto flute. Although this may have been
the case in the past, alto flute literature is currently
gaining in popularity.

The information provided in this section is intended to clarify some issues for the music educator and,
in turn, may encourage more use of the alto flute within
the mainstream of public school music education.

I. WHAT SIZE IS THE ALTO FLUTE? The alto flute is
slightly larger than the concert C flute in both the
size of the bore and the length. Doubling between the
concert C flute and the alto flute is not too difficult
because of almost identical finger spread. Because of
this careful planning, the hand and finger positions are
similar to that of the C flute. Thus, after the student
overcomes the initial awkwardness, switching becomes
easy.

Students should not play the alto flute unless
they have physically matured to the point where they
have large hands and long arms. This usually occurs in
eighth or ninth grade. The increased weight and length
means more breath is needed to produce a full tone.
Selecting a student too early will only hinder this
goal.

II. WHAT IS THE PLAYING RANGE OF THE ALTO FLUTE? The
alto flute is in the key of G. It plays exactly the
same notes as the regular flute even using the same
fingerings, however, the notes played sound four tones
lower than written (see Figure 226).

written   sounds   range of actual
                         sounds

Figure 226. Alto flute range sounds four
tones lower than written.

Each octave has its own unique characteristic, yet the
alto flute is best known for the beauty of its lower
register. The haunting quality of the lower register
is used by numerous television and film makers across
the country. The middle register, however, presents a
problem that is not encountered on the smaller flutes.
With the piccolo, E^b flute, and the concert C flute,
there is evenness of tone quality throughout the range
of the instrument. With the larger flutes, i.e., the
alto and bass, there is a noticeable difference in tone
quality in the middle of the second octave, namely,
between D^2 to F$^{\#2}$ (see Figure 227).

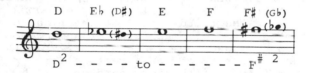

Figure 227. Problem tones for alto flute.

The tonal roughness for the D^2 and the D$^{\#2}$ can be eliminated on all the flutes simply by raising the first
finger of the left hand. When this is done, a small
vent hole is opened. This opening prevents longer
lengths of vibrations from forming in the air column,
almost like splitting the air. By doing this, the
rough sound or natural undertone that forms is avoided.
Thus, raising the first finger of the left hand has become the standard fingering for the entire flute family.
Having students play a D^2 or D$^{\#2}$ the correct way and
then depressing the index finger of the left hand will
easily demonstrate the harsh sound the incorrect finger
produces. The necessity of using the correct fingering
for these tones is important throughout the flute
family (see Figure 228).

Figure 228. Correct fingerings for
D^2 and $D^{\#2}$ for the flute family.

With the smaller flutes, however, no other alternate
fingerings are necessary for the E^2, F^2, and the $F^{\#2}$.
The piccolo, E^b and C flutes are small enough that it
is possible to push enough air through the instrument
quickly enough to avoid any rough sound. On the larger
flutes, this becomes a little more difficult.

Through the years, instrument manufacturers have considered the use of an octave key to remedy this concern,
however, to date, none have been manufactured. An
available option which provides a more balanced scale
is the use of alternate fingerings. Experimentation
has proven that if the $D^{\#}$ trill key (the second trill
key played with the third finger of the right hand) is
used, these notes become much clearer and compatible
with the tones around them (see Figure 229). This works
because the trill key acts as a vent in similar manner
as the first finger of the left hand does with middle D^2
and $D^{\#2}$ (see Figure 228). A few other alternate fingerings that have proven successful for the larger flutes
are provided in Figure 230 (see Figure 230).

Figure 229. Alternate fingerings for E^2,
F^2, and $F^{\#2}$ on the alto flute.

All the fingerings notated in Figures 229 and 230 are
useful and should be used in slow solo passages, octave
skips, or where uniformity of sound is desired among
several flutes. They provide not only a clearer sound
but also one that is closer to that of the regular

flute. These fingerings, however, are rather awkward
in fast passages, therefore, are to be used strictly as
a substitute for regular fingerings.

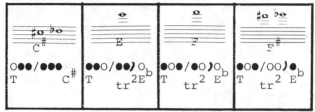

Figure 230. Alternate fingerings
for alto flute.

III. WHAT ARE THE BASIC PRINCIPLES OF TONE PRODUCTION?
The alto flute, like the piccolo, is a compromise. The
embouchure hole on the alto flute is slightly smaller
than it should be because if it were made to fit the
size of the instrument, students would have to use a
great deal of air making it difficult to obtain a sound.
Although the embouchure hole is not the exact size, the
intonation problems are still not as severe as those of
the piccolo with its slightly larger than necessary
embouchure hole. Since the pitch between the alto flute
and the C flute is only a perfect fourth, while that of
the piccolo and the C flute is a complete octave, the
intonation problems are not as noticeable.

The alto flute can produce a very mellow, almost
haunting tone in contrast to the brightness of the
smaller flutes. To obtain this quality in all three
registers, the following must be observed:

STEP 1. Low register. The opening in the lips should
be slightly larger than for the C flute. The main
objective is to get as much air as possible into the
instrument without forcing. Placing as much of the
lower lip as possible on the embouchure plate will help.
Also, the upper lip should be firmly against the teeth
which will help direct the airstream down into the flute.

STEP 2. Middle register. The air should be directed at
a slightly higher angle. The principle is the same as
the regular flute. Be careful not to pinch the lips.
Although it is not detrimental to the smaller flutes,
pinching will cause the tone to crack on the larger
instruments. Sometimes, thinking of directing the airstream more toward the back wall of the embouchure plate
makes the tone less resistant to cracking thus attaining
maximum tonal resonance and response.

153

STEP 3. Upper register. This is a combination of the above. Just remember that as the notes ascend, the jaw extends forward and the upper lip remains close against the teeth. Above all, avoid forcing.

IV. WHAT ARE SOME USES FOR THE ALTO FLUTE? The alto flute was first used in orchestral literature by Stravinsky in Rite of Spring and Ravel's Daphnis and Chloe, Suite No. 2. Today, many arrangers and composers are including its use in television and films to create a haunting quality. The alto flute has grown in popularity because of the professional musician's love for the instrument's beautiful sound.

Educators, too, should consider using the alto flute more. Some educators use it in solo passages where its distinct sound can add to the beauty of the music. Others use the alto flute as a substitute for other instruments, such as the English horn. The alto flute can also be used to add support to low flute passages where the flutist is struggling to play a low C. The alto flute would be playing just an F on the first space which is not difficult to obtain, thus, the low C would have the support necessary to help it resonate. Since the alto flute's best notes are in the lower range, it, too, is good for ensemble and flute choir work.

Overall, the alto flute has numerous uses and should be considered as a possible investment by public schools and those individuals who take flute playing seriously.

BASS FLUTE

BASS FLUTE. The bass flute is the lowest sounding member of the flute family. It was first used in its simplest form in the early 1500's. It's age, however, does not reflect its use because the bass flute still remains a rather uncommon instrument in the United States. Recent interest by American instrument manufacturers has brought the price range down to where it is more affordable, yet, many individuals cite its size and lack of available literature as chief reasons for not purchasing one. To help clarify some of these issues, the following information is presented.

I. WHAT IS THE SIZE OF THE BASS FLUTE? The bass flute is the largest member of the flute family. In its

154

initial development, manufacturers found that to produce the proper sound, the tube would have to be so long
that the instrument would be impossible to hold. To
compensate for this, instrument manufacturers have bent
back the mouthpiece tube to reduce the flute's overall
length to manageable proportions. The mouthpiece is now
alongside the rest of the flute.

The size of the bass flute makes it heavy and
awkward to hold. It often intimidates students creating
more problems than necessary. Instructing students that
the basic playing position is the same as it is for the
other flutes will psychologically assist in making the
instrument feel more comfortable to hold and easier to
play.

II. WHAT IS THE PLAYING RANGE OF THE BASS FLUTE? The
bass flute is in the key of C and sounds an octave lower
than written. It has the same three octave range as the
other members of the flute family (see Figure 231).

written   sounds   range of actual sounds

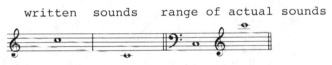

Figure 231. Range of the bass flute.

Each octave has its unique qualities that should be considered when arranging, transposing, or purchasing
music (see Figure 232). Remember, the written note
sounds an octave lower.

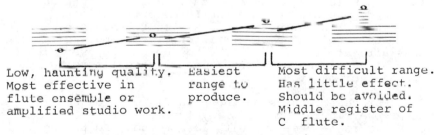

Low, haunting quality.   Easiest   Most difficult range.
Most effective in   range to   Has little effect.
flute ensemble or   produce.   Should be avoided.
amplified studio work.   Middle register of
                                        C flute.

Figure 232. Unique qualities
of the bass flute.

III. WHAT ARE THE BASIC PRINCIPLES OF TONE PRODUCTION?
Because of its large size, the bass flute needs a great
amount of air to produce a full tone. This should be a
primary factor when selecting a child to play one. As

155

a result, embouchure placement becomes critical in order
to make the most efficient use of available breath.
Students often panic when they see the size of the bass
flute and automatically blow harder. This is a fault
that must be quickly overcome because although the flute
is much larger in appearance, it offers less resistance
than the other flutes. The larger bore requires more
breath but not more force. Overblowing will do nothing
more than cause the tone to crack and break into its
upper partials. A summary of key concepts is provided
to insure a full sound in all three registers of the
bass flute. They are:

STEP 1. Low register. The key point here is to open
the mouth as wide as possible and to use a very wide air
stream. Also, bringing the lower jaw back and directing
as much air as possible into the flute should help.
Since a large amount of air is needed in this register
to produce a full sound, students may become a little
tired or dizzy. They should be fine after a short rest
period.

STEP 2. Middle register. The key concept here is to
follow the same principle as with the other flutes,
that is, moving the lower jaw out and changing the air
stream so that less air enters the flute. This is the
easiest range to produce a full sound and one that will
be successfully achieved by most students. As a result,
this is the recommended range to begin students in order
to provide the proper incentive to continue.

STEP 3. Upper register. This is the most difficult
range in which to produce a tone. Most students have
a tendency to blow harder and force out the sound. This
is incorrect because the same procedure should be
followed as with the other flutes, i.e., smaller opening,
less air into the flute. The key point, however, is to
blow as gently as possible. The slightest forcing
causes the tone to crack.

For best results on the bass flute, blow easily,
never overblowing or using any type of force. Remember,
more air is needed, but with less force. Following
these steps should make tone production on the bass
flute much easier.

IV. WHAT ARE SOME USES FOR THE BASS FLUTE? Although in
existence for many years, the bass flute is still not
commonly used. There is little call for it in modern
orchestra and band literature. The best known examples
are in Stravinsky's Rite of Spring and Ravel's Daphnis

and Chloe. Its main use has been with flute choirs, however, it has grown in popularity with jazz, studio, and rock musicians. Recently, there has been a major work for solo bass flute with symphonic band accompaniment by Clifton Williams. Also, Bolling's Suite for Flute and Jazz Piano has boosted the popularity of the instrument.

In the school setting, the bass flute can be used in many different ensembles because it is a non-transposing instrument. Many directors have the bass flute play the lowest part in trio and quartet music. Since it is an octave lower than the C flute, the bass flute adds another interesting tonal harmony and one that is worth exploring.

SUMMARY. It is important for the student to understand that anything playable on any of the other flutes is also playable on the bass flute. To assist in the goal of proper bass flute technique, studies from standard flute literature have proven successful. The bass flute is and will continue to be an important instrument in the field of music.

ONE FINAL POINT. The flute family certainly does provide numerous opportunities for both the educator and the student. With similarities of structure, hand position, embouchure, and fingerings, switching should present no major obstacles. Why not explore these possibilities?

157

APPENDICES (CONT'D)

APPENDIX A

WHAT MAKES THE FLUTE PLAY?

ACOUSTICS. Understanding "why" a flute sounds as it does is extremely important if students expect to become well-rounded musicians. Often, however, instructors avoid this aspect of education judging the "why" is too difficult to explain to their students. This concern is, indeed, justified, especially since an in-depth study of acoustics would be necessary for a better comprehension. Since a complete course in acoustics is beyond the scope of this manual, this section will treat one aspect that is important for a better understanding of the flute sound, namely, harmonics. Consultation of Appendix H, recommended collateral reading, should assist those desiring more detailed information concerning acoustics.

1. FUNDAMENTAL TONES. The tone produced on the flute is caused by the air vibrating inside the tube. The number of times (frequency) the air vibrates is determined by the length of the enclosed air column. With a longer length of tubing, the air vibrates at a slower rate thus producing a lower sound. With a shorter length tubing, the air vibrates at a faster rate thus producing a higher sound. Understanding this aspect, it is apparent that covering all the holes of the flute produces the lowest pitch since it creates the longest length of tubing. Raising the fingers one at a time until all the holes are open, shortens the column of air, thus raising the pitch. These tones produced in the lowest register of the flute are referred to as fundamental tones.

2. HARMONICS. Since the flute is capable of playing several octaves, it is important for the student to understand how these high pitches are produced. To do this, it is helpful to analyze the vibration pattern of a violin string. When an open string is set into vibration, it vibrates more widely in the middle than at the ends. This wide spot is referred to as loops while the ends are called nodes (see Figure 234).

nodes   loops   nodes

Figure 234. Open string vibration pattern.

161

On the flute, the nodes occur in the center while
the loops are at both ends of the tube, however, the
principle remains the same. If the string is touched
gently in the middle, it will vibrate in two equal segments. These segments will be one-half as long as the
string, therefore, will vibrate twice as fast as the
open string. This quicker vibration will produce another tone an octave higher than the tone of the full
length. This tone is referred to as a harmonic.

Since there are several harmonics for each tone,
one individual harmonic is frequently called an overtone
or a partial of the fundamental tone. If the string is
divided into three equal parts, these segments vibrate
three times as fast as the full string producing a tone
a twelfth above the fundamental tone. This is another
harmonic or overtone. To illustrate this, the first
eight partials of a C string are shown in Figure 235
(see Figure 235). The C is the fundamental tone while
the other pitches are overtones of this basic pitch.

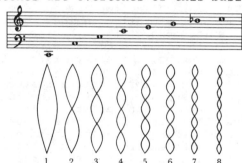

Figure 235.   Overtone series on a C string.

The two upper registers on the flute are basically
harmonics produced by such vibrating segments. Since
these harmonics cannot be produced by simply touching
a string, the woodwinds rely on octave or register keys.
These keys act as vents which make the air column vibrate into segments (partials). Since the flute does
not have a register or octave key, it behaves a little
differently.

To obtain the second register on the flute, the
performer's lower lip acts as the octave key. Since
the fingerings are basically the same as the lower
octave, the flutist must change the direction of the
air so that less air enters the tube. This is done
with the lower lip. The absence of air in the tube is
what causes the air to vibrate differently creating the

162

necessary vibrations to produce the tone in the second octave. The upper register of the flute uses a more complicated system of fingering. These fingerings create vents which further break the column of air into smaller segments which produce the higher pitches.

3. TONE QUALITY. Harmonics, therefore, are a series of tones (partials) which are parts of the main tone (fundamental). The fundamental tone is the strongest tone because all the harmonics are present. Any combination of these overtones has an effect on the overall tone quality (timbre) of the flute. All the overtones are present in the fundamental tone, however, the fundamental drops out when the second register is played. This is what gives a different quality of sound on the flute. Analyzing a tone by the strengths or weaknesses of its overtones will demonstrate how each tone has its own particular quality.

While the general nature of harmonics is a product of the instrument itself, the relative interrelationship between them is controlled by the player. With a better understanding of harmonics, students should be able to produce a more beautiful tone.

APPENDIX B

THE FLUTE'S HISTORY

GENERAL

Any person interested in the flute will find its
history a fascinating subject. Since the flute's
history dates back to ancient times, it becomes impossible to cover all aspects, therefore, this section will
present in logical order some of the most important
facts of interest to the flutist. For those interested
in a more detailed account of the flute's history, consultation of the collateral reading found in Appendix H
is highly recommended.

LEGEND

There are many legends about the flute's discovery,
however, one of the best known concerns the story of
Pan, the Greek god of nature and universe. According to
myth, Pan was chasing the beautiful nymph, Syrinx,
through the forest in hope of capturing her for his
personal pleasures. During the chase, Syrinx ran into
the forest to escape, but to no avail since Pan was in
close pursuit. Syrinx became tired and ran toward a
nearby river. Just as she entered the water, she
realized escape was impossible, thus, prayed to be saved
from Pan. The Naiads, nymphs of the water, heard her
plea and changed Syrinx into a reed just as Pan was
about to throw his arms around her. To his amazement,
Pan discovered that his arms were wrapped around nothing
more than a bunch of reeds.

Pan, breathing a sigh of despair, discovered that
his breath traveling over the reeds produced musical
sounds. Pan soon forgot his disappointment and amused
himself by playing tunes on different size pipes that
he made from the reeds. He called these pipes Syrinx
reeds in honor of the beautiful nymph he was chasing.
Today, these same reeds are referred to as Panpipes
(see Figure 236).

Figure 236. Panpipes

165

THE BEGINNING

Undoubtedly, the flute's real inventor was nature.
Long before recorded history, primitive man probably
heard the wind blowing across a reed and then tried to
imitate the sound by blowing across a similar reed.
Soon after, man discovered that hollow bones were a
good source of sound and eventually added tone holes to
create additional tones. Hollow reindeer foot bones
have been found that are tens of thousands of years old
(see Figure 237).

Figure 237. Reindeer footbone flute.

Similar bones with several tone holes have been
found in Peru dating back to century 100 A.D. (see
Figure 238).

Figure 238. Bone Quena from Peru
(c. 100 A.D.).

ANCIENT TIMES

The flute's recorded history begins with archeolo-
gical findings in ancient tombs. These flute-like
instruments apparently had religious significance since
they were found buried with other valued items. Also,
hollow bones of birds have been found around the
diggings which were probably used as a hunting call for
animals. Too, tubes of varying lengths, blown out at
one end, have been found in Chinese and Egyptian tombs
dating back to 2,000 B.C. As time passed, the primitive
flute had been carried to all continents with each age
and culture contributing to its development. A few of
these are:

1. Primitive flutes. Most early primitive flutes were
a single tube made from wood, reeds, bamboo, bone or
clay. The tone was produced by blowing across the end

of the tube. These are considered the most primitive
form of flute. Pictures have been inscribed on cave
walls dating back to 2,000 B.C.

2. Panpipes. As time passed, ancient Egyptians, limited by a single tone, tried combining single reeds of
varying lengths to create a crude scale. These are
referred to as Panpipes, named after the Greek god, Pan.

3. V-shape cut. Later, ancient people discovered that
by making a V-cut shape out of the edge of the opening,
the tube became easier to play and produced a more
brilliant sound (see Figure 239).

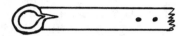

Figure 239. V-cut shape produces
a more brilliant sound.

4. Major improvement. A major improvement occurred
when some unknown person plugged the open end of the
tube with wood and them made a small opening slightly
lower than the piece of wood. This opening had a sharp
edge which produced the tone (see Figure 240).

Figure 240. Edge cut opening.

5. First tone holes. The first tone holes, like most
discoveries with the primitive flute, were probably
discovered by accident. Occasionally, primitive man,
in his crude attempts at making a panpipe or whistle,
tried to enhance it by adding some type of design on it.
One such person may have gone too far cutting a hole
into the tube. Upon playing it, this ancient craftsman
may have noticed that the pitch of the pipe changed.
Too, it was probably discovered that by covering the
hole with the finger, the original pitch was restored.
This may have been the beginning of finger holes. A
three-holed Egyptian flute has been found dating back
to 200 B.C.

6. Double flute. Pictures of double flutes have been
found on old Egyptian paintings. These flutes were

167

nothing more than simple tubes open at both ends but
could produce two tones simultaneously (see Figure 241).

Figure 241.   Double flute.

7.   Other ancient flutes.   Another ancient flute is the
Polynesian nose flute which is not blown by the mouth
but, instead, across the end by the nostril.   The other
nostril not in use is closed by the muscles in the nose.
The player now has the freedom to hum and grunt while
playing.   Globular flutes are egg-shaped, clay flutes
located in Peru.   Air is blown through a small hole
which produces the sound.   Another primitive flute is
the tabor, a three-hole pipe played with one hand,
while the other hand beats a drum.   This primitive flute
was used to accompany dancing.

MIDDLE AGES AND RENAISSANCE 1100-1500.

The changes that took place during this period
were gradual.   The flute was played vertically and was
referred to as a recorder.   It was quite popular among
the medieval troubadours during the 12th Century.   The
horizontal flute first appeared in Europe at the end of
the 13th Century, however, it was not until the 14th
Century that it became accepted.

1660-1775.

Around 1650, the transverse flute was in general
use and other than the flute being blown from the side,
no other major changes were made until 1677.   This flute
was usually made of wood and had six finger holes to
produce the tones (see Figure 242).   The musician was
usually limited to what could be played often resorting
to many crossfingerings in order to play a chromatic
scale.

Figure 242.   Six hole flute.

168

Through experimentation, it became known that a hole between D, the last hole on the flute, and the end of the tube would produce a semitone between the notes D and E, but it was too difficult to cover with the little finger of the right hand. Soon, an unknown flutist hit upon the idea of a key which would enable the little finger to open and close the extra hole with ease. The one key flute, which could now produce the $D^{\#}/E^{b}$ with greater ease, was developed and soon became the standard orchestral flute for the era (see Figure 243).

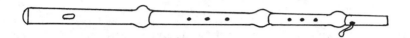

Figure 243. One key flute.

In 1680, interest began with the design of a conical bore flute with a cylindrical headjoint. Prior to this, all flutes were designed with a cylindrical bore. Hotteterre le Romain, a famous flute maker from France, was the first to take interest in its development. Interest in flute design rapidly increased when the first complete treatise on the flute was published by Hotteterre in 1707. Other companies soon began manufacturing one-key flutes such as Bressan of London, Scherer of Paris, and Cahusac of England. In 1726, the tuning cork inserted at the end of the flute headjoint was devised, another remarkable improvement.

1776-1832.

During this period, further changes were made paving the way for the grand inventor, Theobald Boehm. In the year 1776, the famous flutist, Johann Joachim Quantz developed a second key which was placed beside the E^{b} key. In the same year, Potter, a famous London flute maker, extended the range down to low C. With this addition, the three key flute had all the basic principles of today's flute since low C and $C^{\#}$ could now be produced.

Soon, other companies began adding keys in further attempts to eliminate difficult cross fingerings and to improve the tone and intonation of the flute. In 1782, five-key flutes were designed, and by the year 1820, eight-key flutes were being manufactured. Although manufacturers continued to experiment with additional keys, the majority of flutists could not adapt to all the different fingering systems, thus, it was not

169

uncommon to still see one-key flutes being used. At
this point, a very important person entered the scene
who was soon to revolutionize the flute making process.
This man was Theobald Boehm.

1832-Present.

In the year 1831, Nicholson, a famous English flute
virtuoso, gave a concert in London on a seven-key flute.
Present at the concert was Theobald Boehm. Boehm,
being a fine flutist himself, marvelled at Nicholson's
ability. At this point, Boehm, desiring to play better
than Nicholson, decided to rival him with an improved
instrument. Boehm judged that if he could perfect a
flute that would facilitate playing, he would undoubtedly be better than Nicholson.

Up to this point, most instrumental makers were
performers who were dissatisfied with the available
instrument. These musicians attempted to correct the
problems they encountered which were usually only the
one or two they experienced. In most cases, however,
recognizing the need for a better instrument was not
enough to do it. Most of these dissatisfied musicians
did not possess a high level of skill in physics,
engineering, or the operation of a machine shop. Boehm
did, and as a result, he revolutionized the flute.

THEOBALD BOEHM.

Theobald Boehm was born on April 9, 1794, in Munich,
Bavaria. Since he was a rather frail, sickly individual,
with weak lungs, playing the flute helped Boehm overcome
his illness. Consequently, Boehm's interest grew in the
construction of the flute. Since Boehm's father was a
goldsmith, Theobald had all the necessary tools available for the flute's construction. In 1810, at the age
of 16, Boehm constructed a four-key flute which he
played. At 18, Boehm was appointed first flutist with
the Munich Theater. In 1828, Boehm's interest continued
to grow as he founded a factory which manufactured
eight-key flutes. This is the flute Boehm played until
1831 when he heard Nicholson play and decided to con-
struct an entirely new flute.

During his experimentation, the first thing Boehm
noticed was that the finger holes were placed too close
together to give the exact tones. Boehm concluded that
these holes had to be placed this way since the hands
of the flutist would not be large enough to cover
correctly placed holes. Boehm also thought that the

170

sound of the flute was not very loud and attributed
this to the small finger holes. Once again, Boehm
concluded that since no flutist's fingers would be
large enough to cover the holes if made to the correct
size, the holes had to be made small.

To correct these problems, Boehm took two flutes
of the same size. Each flute had an embouchure hole
but no finger holes. Boehm then cut off the end of one
flute until it gave the next higher note of the scale.
After carefully measuring the length of the flute, he
bored a hole at the correct spot on the second flute to
obtain this sound. Boehm then cut off more tubing from
the first flute until the next note was produced. Again,
after careful measurements, Boehm drilled another hole
in the second flute until the pitch was obtained. Boehm
continued to do this until all the necessary holes were
drilled to make a complete chromatic scale. Following
this, Boehm invented a method of opening and closing
keys to cover these holes. Where the fingers would not
reach, Boehm attached keys to a rod so that if a flutist
pressed one key, another could also close. Boehm then
devised a new fingering system to correspond with this
new ring key mechanism. Boehm achieved this goal in
the year 1832, yet this new flute did not receive
immediate acceptance. This was probably due to the new
and difficult fingerings.

In 1838, the French Academy of Fine Arts took an
interest in Boehm's flute and began to test it very
critically. It not only passed all tests, but because
of its excellence, Boehm's flute was universally
adopted by all Parisian conservatories. These results
would have made most individuals extremely happy, but
not so with Boehm. Since his flute was analyzed by
mere opinion and not scientific, mathematical principles,
Boehm could not be satisfied with their conclusions. It
was then that Boehm decided to compute the acoustical
formula for flute construction.

To accomplish this, Boehm conducted over 300 experiments using different materials, bore sizes, shapes
plus numerous locations and sizes of the tone holes.
Boehm conducted all these experiments in accordance with
the laws of physics instead of by trial and error.

As a result of these experiments, Boehm built a
flute that had a cylindrical body which produced a
louder and richer tone. The flute was made of silver
which gave the tone more brilliance. In addition,

Boehm replaced the ring keys with covered keys making the flute much easier to play.

Completed in 1847, Boehm's skill as a performer and composer enabled him to play on his invention and convince the music world of its worth. With some minor alterations, this is the flute used today making Boehm truly the inventor of the modern day flute.

APPENDIX C

NEW TRENDS FOR FLUTES

New performance techniques is an area that is not
only quite vast, but one that is continually growing.
In recent years, more new sound sources and music
notation symbols have been introduced than in any other
period of music history. With this newness, as in any
period of music, there is a feeling of risk and insecur-
ity, not only by the composer who wonders if his work
will be accepted, but also by the performer who is un-
familiar with these new performance techniques. This
worry is compounded by the fact that numerous composers
have their own individual fingerings and special effects
which makes each piece a new and interesting challenge.

To assist the educator and performer, this section
will aim at consolidating these concepts to the most
frequently used modifications of the basic flute sound.
It is hoped that this organization will standardize
these effects somewhat, and assist both the educator and
performer in exploring this new literature with a more
positive attitude.

I. MULTIPHONICS. Sometimes referred to as multiple
sonorities, multiphonics is the technique of producing
two or more pitches simultaneously. To achieve this
effect, the player must spread the airstream over the
embouchure hole as wide as possible. If, for example,
the player fingers F^3, it is possible to also produce
B^{b1} and A^2. This is done by varying the airstream until
the note is achieved. With practice, it is possible to
combine any two or three notes at the same time producing a multiphonic sound (see Figure 244).

using F^3 fingering   With proper spreading of
and spreading air,   air, it is possible to
B^b and A results.   combine pitches.

Figure 244. An example of multiphonics.

Some multiphonics can be played with regular fingerings
while others must use different combinations. Whichever
is the case, composers normally include the fingering

for the multiphonic on the printed page near the note
being played (see Figure 245).

T ●○●/●○○ E^b

Figure 245. Multiphonic fingerings are
usually included on the printed page.

II. PERCUSSIVE EFFECTS. Often contemporary composers
use a percussive effect produced by slapping the keys
down on the flute. Since no air is used with this technique, it has a limited effective range. Normally, C^1
(B^1 if applicable) to G^1, a minor 6th higher, is considered the best range (see Figure 246). For the next
octave, closing the embouchure hole with the curve of
the chin creates a closed pipe which, in turn, helps
the sound to resonate when the keys are slapped (see
Figure 247).

B^1 C^1 G^1

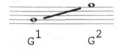

G^1 G^2

Figure 246. Best range
for a percussive effect.

Figure 247. To produce a
percussive effect in this
range, the embouchure hole
must be sealed.

To produce this percussive effect, it is best to finger
the desired note, then raise and slap close the G key
with the fourth finger of the left hand. This is often
referred as "popping" the G key. The "pop" serves the
purpose of increasing the speed of the air through the
tube thereby creating the maximum possible volume. In
addition to "popping" the G key, some composers prefer
to have the player click keys at random not worrying
about the maximum volume attainable. In regard to
notation, there are basically two types of key slaps;
one in which the key is slapped at the sounded pitch,
and the other in which keys are clicked at random (see
Figure 248).

♩ =(key slap at
sounded pitch)
♩ =(click any key at
random)

Figure 248. Two kinds of key slaps.

174

III. EXTENSION OF TRADITIONAL EFFECTS. Often, contemporary composers take traditional effects and expand
them to suit their individual needs. A few of these
are:

1. <u>Microtones</u>. Microtones, normally associated with
string instruments and electronic music, have recently
been used by contemporary composers with wind instruments. A microtone is a pitch lying between chromatic
pitches. It is a fixed pitch half the distance of a
half-step which is musically referred to as a semitone.
Composers usually indicate whether the note is to be
raised a quarter tone or lowered. Once again, fingerings are normally included on the printed page (see
Figure 249).

= (a sharpening
of a quarter
tone)

= (a flattening
of a quarter
tone)

Figure 249. Examples of microtones.

2. <u>Glissandi</u>. In contemporary literature, a glissandi
consists of sliding between pitches within a specific
starting and ending point. This effect can be either
lipped or fingered, however, it is only possible to use
the fingered effect on an open hole flute. To produce
this effect, performers must slide their fingers across
the holes thus raising or lowering the pitch depending
on the instructions of the music (see Figure 250).

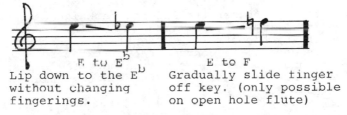

F to E♭
Lip down to the E♭
without changing
fingerings.

E to F
Gradually slide finger
off key. (only possible
on open hole flute)

Figure 250. Lip and finger glissandi.

Wider glissandi are used less frequently. Normally,
this technique is used when it is possible to gradually
slide the fingers of the right hand off the keys simultaneously (see Figure 251).

Figure 251. Typical example
of wider glissandi.

Some less frequently used notations for glissandi are
provided in Figure 252 (see Figure 252).

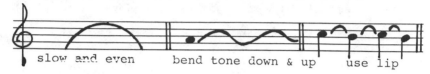

slow and even   bend tone down & up   use lip

Figure 252. Less frequently used glissandi.

3. <u>Flutter tongue</u>. Flutter tonguing is probably the
most commonly used special effect by contemporary composers (see Figure 253). Briefly, it is produced by
rolling the tongue rapidly as if pronouncing the word
"brrrr." For more information concerning the mechanics
of flutter tonguing, consult Section B (Tonguing) of
Chapter IV.

Figure 253. Different ways to notate
flutter tonguing.

4. <u>Vibrato</u>. Another traditional technique extended
beyond its normal use is vibrato. Unlike traditional
music, in which control is essential, vibrato can be as
uneven as desired in contemporary literature. Contemporary vibrato can be produced with both the air and keys.
Instructions are usually provided on the printed page
(see Figure 254).

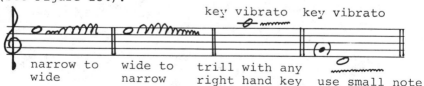

narrow to   wide to   trill with any
wide   narrow   right hand key   use small note

Figure 254. Examples of ways to notate vibrato.

5. Dynamics. In traditional music, dynamics are usually found between the fixed range of pp to ff. Contemporary composers have extended that to such extremes as pppp, mpppp, or fffff. Although there is a definite limit in regard to what level a person can achieve, it is the overexaggeration that produces the desired effect for the contemporary composer (see Figure 255).

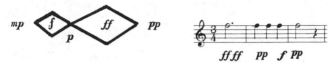

Figure 255. Examples of different ways to indicate dynamics in contemporary literature.

IV. ALEATORIC. Often referred to as the "anything goes" or "chance" music, this technique simply means that the player must improvise with extreme regularity and with as many different manners of attack and articulation as possible. Usually, the notes occur in a downward motion unless specified by the composer (see Figure 256).

| play a note between given note | choose either tone | improvise in approximate range of line | improvise with extreme irregularity |

Figure 256. Examples of aleatoric notation.

V. COLOR FINGERINGS. Contemporary composers use color fingerings when they want to change the quality of any given tone. This changing of timbre is possible when the player changes the regular fingering of a particular note to another fingering. Normally, there are several color fingerings for each note and the composer indicates the desired choice on the printed music (see Figure 257).

Figure 257. Example of a color fingering.

VI. NOVEL REGISTERS. For the flute, contemporary composers have taken the normal three octave range and
extended it an additional fifth (see Figure 258).

Figure 258. Extended flute range.

These notes are rarely used in traditional music,
however, the contemporary performer should be prepared.
These notes are extremely difficult to produce, thus,
only the most advanced player should attempt them. Most
composers include the fingering on the printed music,
however, it is best to know several fingerings for each
note. One fingering may work better than another not
only because of individual differences between players,
but also because the quality of the instrument determines the ease by which these notes are produced. A
few of the extended range fingerings are provided in
Figure 259 (see Figure 259). A more complete list is
provided in Appendix F.

Figure 259. Examples of novel
register fingerings.

VII. USE OF THE MOUTHPIECE. Contemporary composers
have found new uses for the flute mouthpiece. A few of
these are:

1. Siren effect. To produce the siren effect, the
player must remove the headjoint from the flute, place
a finger into the open end, and while blowing air
across the embouchure hole, move the finger in and out.
Depending on the speed of the finger, various siren
effects can be produced. The normal notation for this
is given in Figure 260 (see Figure 260).

178

Siren effect on mouthpiece

Figure 260. Normal notation
for the siren effect.

2. Swooish effect. This effect is very similar to the
burst of air that a player uses to warm up the instrument. To achieve this effect, the player must depress
all the keys, cover the embouchure hole with the lips
and then blow a burst of air into the instrument. The
swooish effect will be heard usually with a downward
glissando due to the rapid exhalation of air (see
Figure 261).

Figure 261. Typical notation
for the swooish effect.

3. Buzz effect. This effect is accomplished by placing
the lips over the mouthpiece embouchure hole and buzzing
into it similar to that of playing a brass instrument
(see Figure 262).

Figure 262. Example of the buzz effect.

4. Other mouthpiece effects. Contemporary composers,
too, ask performers to create other types of air sounds
with the aid of the mouthpiece. One effect is accomplished by blowing or drawing air from the instrument.
To do this, the performer must once again cover the
embouchure hole with the lips and inhale and exhale air
into the instrument in a more controlled manner than the
swooish effect (see Figure 263).

179

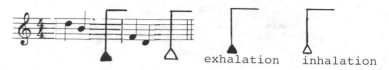

exhalation   inhalation

Figure 263. Example of a more
controlled swooish effect.

One last effect worth mentioning is playing any note on
the headjoint when requested. There is usually a rest
preceding this effect in order to give the player an
opportunity to take the mouthpiece off (see Figure 264).

blow on mouthpiece

Figure 264. Example of playing a note
at any given time, on the headjoint.

VIII. SINGING INTO THE FLUTE. Although used a lot in
jazz, contemporary composers have begun to use the
special effect of singing into the flute with relative
success. Basically, this technique involves the singing
and playing of notes simultaneously. With practice, it
is possible to sing a line completely independent of the
notated music. This singing is basically a hum produced
by keeping the vocal cords tight enough so that they
vibrate as air passes them on its way to the flute (see
Figure 265).

sing
play

hmm

Figure 265. Voice over flute.

IX. SPEAKING INTO THE FLUTE. Contemporary composers
frequently use speaking into the flute as an effective
tool. This is accomplished by rolling the embouchure
hole in toward the lips and pronouncing a variety of
sounds (see Figure 266).

speak pezz

Figure 266. Speaking into the flute.

180

SUMMARY. Although the effects described in this
Appendix may appear confusing to the novice, it is not
an insurmountable task to learn these techniques. Too,
music educators must investigate these new sonorities
in order to keep their knowledge of contemporary
literature current thereby becoming better able to help
their students. This chapter is intended to encourage
more musicians to explore this exciting world of music.

For those desiring a more detailed account of contemporary trends, consult listing under contents of
Appendix H.

FLUTE CHOIRS

WHAT TO DO WITH ALL THOSE FLUTES? The flute today is, indeed, a very popular instrument. Often, there are so many flutes in an organization that there is not enough music to go around. More important, as a result of these large numbers, balance is uneven, students do not receive proper individual attention, there is a reliance on the first chair students by weaker players, and numerous intonation problems crop up that could be eliminated with a smaller section. What should music educators do with all these flutes in order to provide them with a good education?

FLUTE'S POPULARITY. The flute's popularity is largely due to the fact that it is such a flexible instrument. Its pleasing sound appeals to both young and old and it can be used in such musical styles as jazz, folk, Latin, rock, classical, and contemporary. As a result, frequently there are more students taking lessons each year on the flute than on any other single instrument. Once again, what should music educators do with all those flutes in order to provide students with a good music education?

DIRECTOR'S DILEMMA. Even with the increase of flutes, the music educator still has the responsibility of providing playing and learning opportunities for those students whether or not all of them can be used in any one particular organization. What is an effective way to accomplish this task?

FLUTE CHOIRS. Many music educators have turned to flute choirs to solve this dilemma and with a great deal of success. The instrumentation they use varies depending on the availability of flutes within their organization or the particular requirements of the composer, however, the full ensemble uses at least one of each of the following instruments:

1. piccolo in C
2. E^b soprano flutes
3. concert C flutes
4. alto flute in G
5. bass flute in C

Those schools that have the complete instrumentation are fortunate, however, not having all of them is no need for despair because alternate instruments can be used. For instance, if a school does not have an alto or bass flute, rewriting the part for the alto and bass clarinet provides not only a beautiful sound but also gives the alto and bass clarinet players a chance to perform more than supporting roles within an organization. Too, there is a great deal of trio music available that uses three flutes, or piccolo and two flutes, etc. Taking this music and doubling the parts also gives the effect of a choir and gives more students an opportunity to perform.

POSITIVE ASPECTS OF FLUTE CHOIR. To further enhance the possibility of beginning and justifying the use of a flute choir, consider these selling points:

POINT 1. In most flute choirs, there is only one player on a particular part. As a result, most students find themselves practicing their music harder in order not to be embarrassed by their peers. Thus, the flute choir tends to strengthen weaker players and helps them to develop a sense of independence and responsibility that is not possible in larger ensembles.

POINT 2. During most rehearsals, there is never enough time to teach all the different aspects of performance necessary to develop a well-rounded student. Choir experience provides the opportunity for the student to experience and the educator to discuss such items as tone, intonation, vibrato, etc., which can be applied to the full ensemble rehearsal.

POINT 3. Through the flute choir, alto and bass flutes can be taught and then applied to the full band.

POINT 4. The flute choir can adapt to most situations since its size can vary from three, as in a trio, to a full flute choir instrumentation.

POINT 5. Provides an excellent opportunity in giving as many flute players as possible ensemble experience.

POINT 6. Provides more solo work for stronger players which motivates them in further developing their skills.

POINT 7. The flute choir is a unique ensemble that will provide the audience with a new and different listening experience.

POINT 8. Provides a better basis from which to teach good flute sound without the distraction of the brass,

percussion, strings, or any of the other woodwind
instruments.

PERFORMANCE TECHNIQUES. Most flute choirs stand while
performing. If, however, a lengthy program is planned,
ensembles may find it more convenient to sit. Whichever
method is used, the formation should be in a semi-circle.
Some educators prefer the higher pitched instrments on
the left and the lower pitched instruments to the right
while others prefer the opposite. Whatever the preference, it is most important that the instrumentation
appears in a consecutive order without any break in the
tonal range of the flutes. This seems to give the best
blend and provides the performer and listener with a
good experience (see Figure 267).

Figure 267. Suggest playing
position for flute choirs.

MUSIC. The following list of available flute choir
literature is only a partial list. It is in no way
intended to be complete, especially with the new music
that is constantly available. The list is to serve as
an introduction. For a more complete list, the reader
should consult James Pellerite's <u>Literature for the
Flute</u>, a Zalo publication, second edition.

COMPOSER/ARRANGER	TITLE/PUBLISHER/INSTRUMENTATION	GRADE
Albert, Morris	Feelings, Hansen piccolo, 4 flutes, optional string bass, optional alto flute	III
Bach, J. S.	Air from the Suite in D Major, Southern 4 flutes and alto, bass flute can be added	III
Bach, J. S.	Minuet, Berwin 4 C flutes	I
Beerman, Burton	Frame for Six Flutes, Southern 6 flutes of which 2 double piccolo and 1 doubles alto flute	V-VI
Berlioz-Rearick	Fugue for Two Choirs, Studio 2 choirs of 4 flutes each	IV
Brown, Rayner	Three Fugues for Five Flutes, Western 3 C flutes, 2 alto flutes	IV
Boismortier, J.F.	Six Concertos for Five Flutes, Hofmeister 5 C flutes	IV
Cavally, Robert	Eight Madrigals for Seven Flutes, Southern 7 C flutes, doubling parts for E^b and alto flutes.	IV
Faure, Gabriel	Pavanne, Zalo 4 C flutes with optional alto and bass flutes, string bass and guitar	III
Fuerstner, Carl	Berceuse, Zalo 4 C flutes - 4th part can be played on alto flute	III
Fuerstner, Carl	First Quartet, Southern 4 C flutes	IV
Gabrieli, Antonio	Sonata Piano Forte, Presser 8 C flutes, 1st flute doubles piccolo, 8th flute doubles alto flute	III
Giltay, Berend	Divertimento for Five Flutes, Peters 5 C flutes	IV
Grimm, Hugo	Divertimento for Eight Flutes, Southern 6 C flutes, E^b flute, alto flute	IV
Handel, G. F.	Sarabanda, Southern	IV
Johnson, Bruce	I Write the Songs, Hansen piccolo, 4 C flutes, optional string bass and alto flute	IV

COMPOSER/ARRANGER	TITLE/PUBLISHER/INSTRUMENTATION	GRADE
Kuhlau, Frederick	Grand Quartet in E, Southern 4 C flutes	V
Levi, William	Flute Flirtation, Willis 4 C flutes	II
Luening, Otto	Sonority Canon for Flutes, Highgate 2 to 37 flutes	V
Missal, Joshua	Rondo-Caprice, Leblanc Corp. 6 C flutes, 6th flute doubles on alto	IV
Maury, Lowndes	Changes for Seven Flutes, Avant piccolo, 5 C flutes, alto flute	IV
Praag, Henri	Sonata for Five Flutes, Peters 5 C flutes	IV
Read, Gardner	Sonoric Fantasia No. 3, Op. 125, Seesaw piccolo, E^b flute, C flute, alto flute, bass flute, harp, percussion	V
Silver, Horace	The Preacher, Hansen 4 C flutes, optional alto flute and string bass	III
Tchaikovsky, P.	March Miniature, Southern 2 piccolos, 7 C flutes, alto flute	III
Wagner, T. F.	Under the Double Eagle, Southern 3 C flutes, alto flute	III

APPENDIX E

FLUTE REPERTOIRE

Today, music educators must be familiar with all
types of flute literature. They must be able to choose
music that will not only help young musicians grow, but
also continue the growth of more advanced players.
Educators should provide a balanced, uninterrupted program of study consisting of appropriate methods, solos,
and ensemble materials. Educators, frequently over-
looking the importance of this, hinder the progress of
talented students.

Another aspect often ignored is the importance of
students having a basic repertoire ready to perform at
any given time. Educators frequently wait until students are more advanced before attempting solos, however
those students who have a basic performing repertoire
ready to play on notice receive numerous opportunities
that others must pass up. The importance of building a
repertoire as early as possible in a student's musical
career simply cannot be overstated.

Small ensembles such as duets, trios, and quartets
are also important in a student's musical growth. Often
overlooked by educators, this type of ensemble playing
helps students become more conscious of their playing.
Ensembles almost force students to become more aware of
their intonation, dynamics, and tone color, especially
if they desire to blend and become an integral part of
the ensemble. This will give weaker players an opportunity to imitate their partners' style, articulation,
and phrasing thus acquiring technique that may take
years to learn on a one-to-one basis with an instructor.
Students often playing alone can get by with uneven
rhythms, but performing with a small ensemble helps to
control this and demonstrates the importance of having
accurate rhythms. Ensemble playing is important for
the reasons stated, however, even if one eliminated
these reasons, ensembles should still be encouraged just
for the pure fun and enjoyment that it provides.

Since the flute is one of the oldest woodwind
instruments, there is an overwhelming amount of music
available at all levels of performance. Educators may
find themselves asking what music they should suggest
for their students. The following represents only a
partial list of the music available, however, it is one

189

which has proven most successful for this author. An
attempt has been made to include music representative
of each musical period. The music is graded according
to the following scale:

      I .. Very Easy: Beginners, Elementary

     II .. Easy: Elementary

   III .. Medium Easy: Junior High

    IV .. Medium Difficult: Junior High

     V .. Difficult: High School

    VI .. Very Difficult: Advanced High School,
                               College

   VII .. Virtuoso: College, Professional

By providing the scale above, it is hoped that
educators will be able to draw upon appropriate literature for their students' particular level. For a more
complete list, it is suggested that consultation be
made of Frans Vester's Flute Repertoire Catalogue,
published by Rubank of Chicago, 1967, or James J.
Pellerite's A Handbook of Literature for Flute, 2nd
Edition, Revised, Zalo Publication, 1965.

METHODS

COMPOSER	TITLE	PUBLISHER
Anzalone, V.	Breeze Easy Method, Bk. I	M. Witmark
Cavally, R.	Original Melodious and Progressive Studies	Southern
Eck, E.	Method for Flute, Bk. I	Belwin
Eck, E.	Tone Development for Flute	Belwin
Herfurth, C.	A Tune a Day	Boston
Moyse, M.	Beginner Flutist	Leduc
Soussman, H.	Soussman Method, Bk. I	C. F. Peters
Voxman, H.	Elementary Method	Rubank

SOLOS WITH PIANO ACCOMPANIMENT OR FLUTE ALONE

Anderson, J.	Die Blumen	Southern
Bach, J. S.	Andante	Southern
Bach, J. S.	Minuet	Belwin
Cavally, R.	Solos for the Debutante Flutist	Southern
Doppler, F.	Berceuse	Southern
Elgar, E.	Pomp and Circumstance, Op. 39, No. 1	Carl Fisher
Gluck, C.	Gavotte, from Armide	Schirmer
Handel, G.	Bouree and Minuet	Rubank
Leeuven, A.	Seven Artistic Solos	Southern
Lewallen, J.	Andantino	Belwin
Mozart, W.	Adagio	Belwin
Rose, D.	Holiday for Flutes	Conn
Rouseel, A.	Aria	Leduc
Tremais, J.	Sarabunde and Minuet	C. F. Peters
Weber, F.	The Peasant Dance	Belwin

DUETS

Collection/Ed. Arnold, J.	Easy Flute Solos or Duets No. 102	Amsco
Collection/Ed. Stouffer, P.	Duets for Two Flutes	Henri Elkan

COMPOSER	TITLE	PUBLISHER
Garibaldi, G.	Six Little Duets, Op. 145	Cundy-Bettoney
Schaeffer	Duets are Fun	Pro Art

TRIOS

Collection/Ed. Wilkins, F.	Flute Sessions	Shawnee
Collection/Ed. Hudadoff	24 Flute Trios	Pro Art
Harris, F.	Petite Mazurka	Ludwig
Lester, L.	So Easy Trios	Boston

QUARTETS

Bach, J. S.	Minuet	Belwin
Collection/arr. Buchtel-Pascherdag	First Ensemble Book for Four Flutes	Neil Kjos
Collection/arr. Holmes, G.	Flute Symphony	Rubank
Gosseo, F.	Gavotte	Belwin

LEVEL II

METHODS

Altes	Complete Method	C. F. Peters
Cavally, R.	Melodious and Progressive Studies Bk. I	Southern
Garibaldi, G.	30 Easy and Progressive Studies Bk. I	Southern
Pares	Pares Scale Studies	Belwin
Platanov, N.	School of Flute Playing	Leeds
Skornicka, J.	Intermediate Method	Rubank
Soussman, H.	Soussman, Bk. 2	C. F. Peters
Wagner	Foundation to Flute Playing	C. F. Peters

SOLOS FOR FLUTE WITH PIANO ACCOMPANIMENT

Alwyn, W.	Three Easy Pieces	Mills
Bach, J. S.	Bourree, from Suite in B Minor	Schirmer
Cavall, R.	24 Short Concert Pieces	Southern

COMPOSER	TITLE	PUBLISHER
Collection/Ed. Arnold, J.	Easy Flute Solos, Everybody's Favorites #83	Amsco
Collection/Ed. D'Andrie, F.	Five Pieces	Leeds
Collection/Ed. Moyse, L	40 Little Pieces for Beginner Flutist	Schirmer
Handel, G. F.	Seven Sonatas and Famous Largo	Southern
Mozart, W.	Two Sonatinas	C. F. Peters
Ravel, M.	Berceuse	Durand
Telemann, G.	Fifteen Pieces	C. F. Peters
Telemann, G.	Suite in A Minor	Southern

DUETS

Collection/Ed. Carey, M.	Flute Duet Album	Belwin
Collecion/ Voxman, H.	Selected Duets, Vol. I	Rubank
Cossec, F.	Gavotte for Two Flutes and Piano	Carl Fisher
Schubert, F.	Five Little Duets	Mercury

TRIOS

Cacavas, J.	Shimmering Flutes	Southern
Cohan, G. M.	Yankee Doodle Dandies	Belwin
Collection/ Voxman, H.	Chamber Music for Three Flutes	Rubank
Mozart, W. A.	Larghetto and Minuetto	Belwin
Witt, C. F.	Suite in ? Major	Carl Fisher

QUARTETS

Collection/arr. Arnold-Lindsay	Flute Quartets, Everybody's Favorites, #121	Amsco
Collection/arr. Gearhart-Wilkins	Flute Sessions	Shawnee
Gluck, C.	Andante and Caprice	Rubank
Scarlatti, A.	Aria and Minuet	Rubank

LEVEL III

METHODS

Anderson, J.	24 Small Caprices, Op. 37	International
Anderson, J.	18 Studies for Flute, Op. 41	International
Berbiguier	18 Studies	C. F. Peters
Cavally, R.	Melodious and Progressive Studies Bk. 2	Southern
Garibaldi, G.	30 Easy and Progressive Studies Bk. II	Augener
Moyse, M.	24 Etudes Petites Melodious	Leduc
Woods, D.	Studies for Upper Notes	C. F. Peters

SOLOS WITH PIANO ACCOMPANIMENT OR FLUTE ALONE

Anderson, J.	Scherzino	Rubank
Bach, J. S.	Adagio, from Toccato and Fugue in C Major	Southern
Bennett, R.	A Flute at Dusk	Boosey & Hawkes
Cavally, R.	15 Concert Pieces for Flute	Southern
Collection/Ed. Arnold, J.	Flute Solos, Everybody's Favorite No. 38	Amsco
Collection/Ed. Voxman, H.	Concert and Contest Collection	Rubank
Debussy, C.	Minuet	Durand
Donjon, J.	Petite Pieces Pastorales	Presto
Fils, A.	Concerto in D Major	Southern
Handel, G.	Seven Sonatas and Famous Largo	Southern
Maler, W.	Small Elegie for Flute Alone	Baerenreiter
Mozart, W. A.	Concerto in D Major	Southern
Scarlatti, A.	Two Sinfonias, F Major and G Major	Muller
Telemann, G.P.	Concerto in G Major	International

DUETS

Barre, M.	Suite in G	Ricordi
Beethoven, L.	Allegro and Minuet	C. F. Peters
Collection	The Favorite Flute Solos	Cundy-Bettoney
Collection/Ed. Guenther, R.	Masterworks for Two Flutes, Vol. I and II	Belwin

194

COMPOSER	TITLE	PUBLISHER
Handel, G. F.	Sonata for Two Flutes	Southern
Koehler, E.	Forty Progressive Duets	Carl Fisher
Loeillet, J.B.	Sonata in C Minor	International
Moyse, M.	Album of Thirty Duets	International
Quantz, J. J.	Sonata in G Major	International

TRIOS

Anderson, J.	Scherzino, Op. 55, No. 6	Rubank
Brooke, A.	The Three Musketeers	Cundy-Bettoney
Brown, N.	Doll Dance	Miller
Collection/Ed. Elkan, H.	Ensemble Trio Album	C. F. Peters
Jacobson, I.	Three Flights for Flutes	Mills
Telemann, G.P.	Sonata in B^b Major	E. F. Peters

QUARTETS

Anderson, J.	Valsette	Belwin
Collection/arr. Voxman, H.	Quartet Repertoire	Rubank
Koehler, E.	Scherzo	Rubank
Rose, D.	Holiday for Flutes	Conn
Rubinstein, A.	Valse Staccato, Op. 23	Belwin

LEVEL IV

METHODS

Cavally, R.	Melodious and Progressive Studies, Bk. III	Southern
Demersseman	50 Melodious Studies, Op. 4, Bk.II	Leduc
Drouet, L.	25 Etudes for Flute	Leduc
Garibaldi, G.	20 Etudes, Op. 132	International
Miramont	15 Technical Studies	Southern
Moyse, M.	Exercise Journaliers	Leduc
Schade	24 Caprices	Southern

SOLOS WITH PIANO ACCOMPANIMENT OR FLUTE ALONE

Arrieu, C.	Sonatina	International

COMPOSER	TITLE	PUBLISHER
Bach, C.P.E.	Sonata in A Minor for Flute Alone	Southern
Bach, J.	Sonata No. 3 in G Major	International
Beethoven, L.	10 Variations on Airs, Op. 107	International
Caplet, A.	Reverie and Petite Valse	Southern
Collection/Ed. Cambers	Essential Repertoire for Flute	Universal
Collection/ International	Contemporary French Recital Pieces	International
Debussy, C.	Syrinx for Flute Alone	Southern
Faure, G.	Fantaisie, Op. 79	Southern
Godard, B.	Suite for Flute and Piano, Op. 116	Carl Fisher
Krol, B.	Pastorella, Op. 24 for Flute Alone	Bote and Bock
Loeillet, J.	Sonata in G Minor	International
Marcello, B.	Sonatas in F Major, D Minor and C Major	Baerenreiter
Mozart, W. A.	Concerto in G Major	Southern
Reichardt, J.F.	Sonata	Southern
Telemann, G.	Concerto in C Minor	Schott

DUETS

Alboni, T.	Three Sonatas	Schott
Bennett, R.	Conversations	Universal
Berbiquier, T.	Six Easy Duets, Op. 59	International
Boismortier, J.	Sonata for Two Flutes, Op. 6, No. 6	International
Buchner, F.	Six Duets	C. F. Peters
Collection/Ed. Wilkins, F.	Flute Sessions	Shawnee
Collection/ Voxman, H.	Selected Duets, Vol. II	Rubank
Devienne, F.	Six Sonatas	International
Quantz, J. J.	Sonata in C Major	International
Soussman, H.	Twelve Pieces for Two Flutes, Op. 47	International
Telemann, G.P.	Six Sonatas for Two Flutes	International
Tulou, J. L.	3 Duos, Op. 102	C. F. Peters

COMPOSER	TITLE	PUBLISHER

TRIOS

Beethoven, L.	Theme and Variations, Op. 25	Belwin
Berbiquier, T.	Trios for Flutes, Op. 51, No. 1 and No. 2	Southern
Gabrieli, G.	Sonata	C. F. Peters
Haydn, F. J.	Three Trios	International
Loeillet, J.	Concerto in D Major	C. F. Peters
Quantz, J. J.	Sonata in D Major	Associated
Telemann, G.P.	Quartetto in G Major	C. F. Peters

QUARTETS

Collection/arr. Eck.	Quartet for Flutes	Belwin
Jongen, J.	Elegie	Southern
McKay, G.	Christmas Morning Suite	Southern

LEVEL V

METHODS

Cavally, R.	Famous Flute Studies and Duets	Southern
Donjon	The Modern Flutist	Southern
Galli	30 Exercise, Op. 100	Ricordi
Garibaldi, G.	Grand Etudes de Style Op. 134	Southern
Hugues, L.	24 Studies for Flute	International
Karg-Elert	30 Caprices from the Modern Flutist	Southern
Koehler, E.	12 Medium Studies, Op. 33, Bk. II	Carl Fisher
Reichart	Seven Daily Exercises	

SOLOS WITH PIANO ACCOMPANIMENT AND FLUTE ALONE

Abel, K.	Sonata in G Major	Southern
Albinoni, T.	Concerto in G	Ricordi
Beethoven, L.	Serenade, Op. 25	C. F. Peters
Benker, H.	Bavardage for Flute Alone	Breitkopf and Hartel
Blavet, M.	Concerto in A Minor	Ricordi
Chopin, F.	Etude in F Minor	Southern
Couperin, F.	Concert Royal No. 4	International

COMPOSER	TITLE	PUBLISHER
Gaubert, P.	Nocturne and Allegro Scherzando	Southern
Haydn, F. J.	Concerto in D	Associated
Ibert, J.	Piece for Flute Alone	Leduc
Loeillet, J.B.	Sonata in G Minor, Op. 3, No. 3	Schott
Quantz, J. J.	Concerto in D Major	Forbert
Rimsky-Korsakoff	Flight of the Bumble Bee	Willis
Stamitz, K.	Concerto in G Major	Associated
Varese, E.	Denisty 21.5 for Flute Alone	Ricordi
Vivaldi, A.	Concerto in C Minor	International

DUETS

Arrieu, C.	Duo	Amphion
Bach, J. S.	Fifteen Two-Part Inventions	C. F. Peters
Bach, W. F.	Sic Duets for Two Flutes, Vol. I	Associated
Collection/Ed. Taylor, L.	The Flutist's Classic Duet Repertoire	Witmark
Genzmer, H.	Sonata in F$^{\#}$ Minor	Schott
Koehler, E.	Forty Progressive Duets, Vol.II, Op. 55	Carl Fisher
Kuhlau	Three Duets, Op. 81	Carl Fisher
Mozart, W. A.	Six Duets for Two Flutes	C. F. Peters
Petrassi, G.	Dialogo Angelico	Zerboni
Quantz, J. J.	Six Duets, Op. 2, Vol. I	Associated
Rossi, M.	Andantino and Allegro	International
Schwartz, E.	Sibling Suite	Media
Soussman, H.	Twelve Duets, Op. 53	International
Tulou, J.	Six Duets, Etudes	Carl Fisher

TRIOS

Barrere, G.	Deux Pieces Breves	Carl Fisher
Berbiguier, T.	Trio for Flutes, Op. 51, No. 3	Southern
Kuhlau, F.	Trois Grands Trios, Op. 86	International
Tchaikowsky, P.	Danse des Mirlitons	Rubank

COMPOSER	TITLE	PUBLISHER

QUARTETS

Leevwen, A.	Four MINIATURES	Southern
Reicha, A.	Sinfonico, Flute Quartet, Op.12	Cundy-Bettoney
Turecheck, E.	Flute Quintet in D Minor	C. F. Peters

LEVEL VI

METHODS

Anderson, J.	24 Etudes Artistiques, Op. 15	Southern
DiLorenzo, L.	L-Indispensible Bk. I and II	C. F. Peters
Furstenau, A.	17 Grande Etudes	Southern
Koehler, E.	Romantic Etudes, Op. 66	Southern
Koehler, E.	School of Velocity, Op. 77	C. F. Peters
Moyse, M.	Daily Exercises	Leduc
Platanov, N.	30 Studies for Flute	International
Tersehak, A.	Daily Exercises, Op. 71	Southern

<u>SOLOS WITH PIANO ACCOMPANIMENT AND FLUTE ALONE</u>

Abel, K.	Sonata in E. Major	Southern
Bach, C.P.E.	Concerto in D Minor	Associated
Bach, J. S.	Suite in B Minor	Boosey & Hawkes
Bennett, D.	Sonatina for Flute Alone	Universal
Blavet, M.	Six Sonatas	Rudall
Briccialdi, G.	Carnival of Venice	Ludwig
Coppola, C.	Flute Flight	Conn
Doppler, F.	Fantasie	Belwin
Enscoe, G.	Cantabile et Presto	International
Gaubert, P.	Sonata No. 1	Durand
Gaubert, P.	Fantaisie	Southern
Haydn, J. M.	Concert for Flute	Mozart Press
Honegger, A.	Danse de la Chevre for Flute Alone	Senart
Loeillet, J.B.	Sonata in C Minor, Op. 3, No. 4	Schott
Molique, W. B.	Concerto in D Minor, Op. 69	Southern
Quantz, J. J.	Concerto in D Major	Baerenreiter
Roussel, A.	Joueurs de Flute, Op. 27	Durand

COMPOSER	TITLE	PUBLISHER
Taffanel, P.	Andante Pastoral and Scherzettino	Southern

DUETS

Bach, J. S.	Sonata in C Major	Associated
Bach, W. F.	Six Duets for Two Flutes, Vol. II	Associated
Berbiquier, T.	Three Duo Concertants, Op. 11	International
Cage, J.	Three Pieces for Flute Duet, 1935	C. F. Peters
Goeb, R.	2 Divertimenti	C. F. Peters
Kuhlau, F.	Three Duos Concertants, Op. 165	International
Kuhlau, F.	Three Duos Concertants, Op. 87	International
Michael, F.	Gingko	Associated
Quantz, J. J.	Six Duets, Op. 2, Vol. II	Associated
Telemann, G.P.	Six Sonatas for Two Flutes	Carl Fisher

TRIOS

Andre, A.	Original Trio, Op. 27	Belwin
Beethoven, L.	Grand Trio for Three Flutes, Op.87	Southern
Mercadante, S.	Three Serenades	Belwin
Telemann, G.P.	Quartet in D Minor	C. F. Peters

QUARTETS

DiLorenzo, L.	Capriccio, Op. 82, No. 3	C. F. Peters
Kronke, E.	Paraphrase on an Original Theme, Op. 184	C. F. Peters
Lauber, J.	Visions de Corse, Op. 54	C. F. Peters

LEVEL VII

METHODS

Anderson, J.	24 Etudes, Op. 15	Southern
Anderson, J.	24 Etudes, Op. 30	Southern
Anderson, J.	24 Technical Studies, Op. 63	Southern
Anderson, J.	24 Virtuosity Studies, Op. 60	Southern
Briccialdi, G.	6 Grand Studies, Op. 31	Ricordi
Garibaldi, G.	Etudes Mignonnes, Op. 131	Southern
Koehler, E.	8 Difficult Studies, Op. 33	Southern

COMPOSER	TITLE	PUBLISHER
Kuhlau	6 Divertissements	International
Moyse, M.	48 Etudes de Virtuosity	Leduc
Moyse, M.	25 Etudes of Virtuosity based on Czerny	Leduc
Peichler, A.	40 Grand Studies	International

SOLOS WITH PIANO ACCOMPANIMENT OR FLUTE ALONE

Arrieu, C.	Concerto in G	Amphion
Aubert, L.	Introduction and Allegro	Durand
Bach, J. S.	Partita in A Minor for Flute Alone	Southern
Beversdorf, T.	Sonata 1964	Southern
Bozza, E.	Image for Flute Alone	Leduc
Chaminade, C.	Concertino, Op. 107	International
Ganne, L.	Andante et Scherzo	International
Griffes, C. T.	Poem	Schirmer
Guarnieri, C.	Three Improvisations for Flute Alone	Southern
Hindemith, P.	Sonata, 1936	Schott
Ibert, J.	Jeux, Sonatine	Leduc
Piston, W.	Sonata	Associated
Poulenc, F.	Sonata	Schirmer
Prokofieff, S.	Sonata, Op. 94	Leeds
Quantz, J. J.	Sonata No. 4 in D Major	C. F. Peters
Riegger, W.	Suite for Flute Alone, Op. 8	Presser

DUETS

Cimarosa, D.	Concerto in G Major	Southern
Hindemith, P.	Canonic Sonatino, Op. 31, No. 3	Schott
Kuhlau, F.	Tre Duetti Brillianti, Op. 80	Ricordi
Migot, G.	Six Little Preludes, Vol. I and II	Leduc

TRIOS

Albisi, A.	Miniature Suite, No. 1	Cundy-Bettoney
Kuhlau, F.	Trois Trois, Op. 13	Southern
Kuhlau, F.	Grand Trio, Op. 90	Southern

COMPOSER	TITLE	PUBLISHER
	QUARTETS	
Bozza, E.	Jour D'Ete A La Montagne	Leduc
DiLorenzo, L.	I Sequaci di Pan, Op. 32	C. F. Peters
Koehler, E.	Grand Quartet, Op. 92	Cundy-Bettoney
Kuhlau, F.	Grand Quartet in E. Minor	Southern
Sollberger, H.	Grand Quartet	MdGinnis & Mars
	ORCHESTRAL STUDIES	
Brooke, Arthur	Orchestral Studies for Flute	International
Madatov	Orchestral Studies for Flute Bk. I and II	Leeds
Prill, E.	Orchestral Studies for Flute	Southern
Smith, W.	Orchestral Studies for Flute Part I, II, III	United
Strauss, R.	Orchestral Studies from Symphonic Works	International

APPENDIX F

FLUTE FINGERING CHARTS

The flute is an octave instrument. Students should remember that the lower two octaves use basically the same fingerings. While other woodwind instruments have register and octave keys to help the upper tones, the flute does not. These tones can only be produced by changing the embouchure and breath support.

Included in this section are charts for regular, fourth octave, harmonic, trill and pianissimo fingerings. Where applicable, an asterisk will indicate optional fingerings which may be used depending on the judgment of the teacher or the player. These are referred to as alternate fingerings.

HOW TO READ THIS CHART

1. ● - solid color indicates key to be pressed.
2. o - indicates open hole.
3. When a specific key is given, refer to picture for additional help.
4. Fingerings will be given either vertically or horizontally.
5. Where more than one fingering is given, the first is the normal fingering. All others are alternate fingerings that should be used at the discretion of the teacher or player.
6. The optional low B is included.

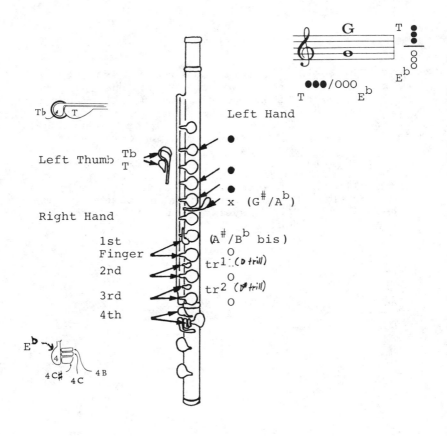

FOURTH OCTAVE FINGERINGS

HARMONIC FINGERINGS

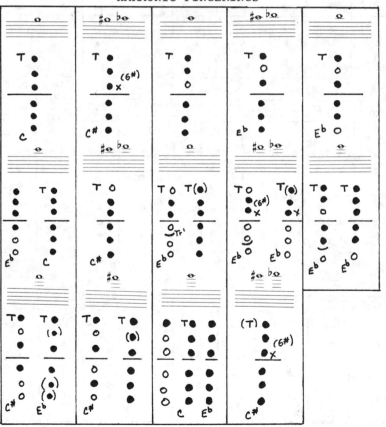

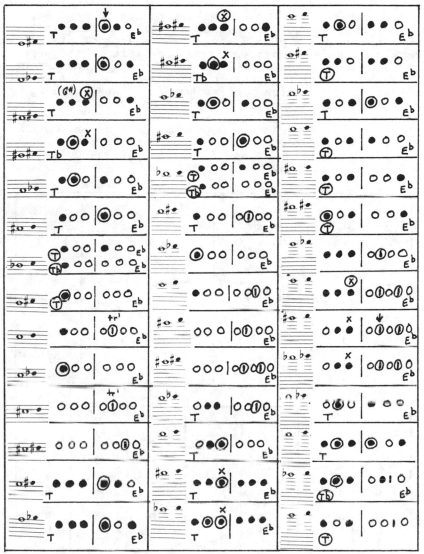

NOTE: Keys to be trilled are circled. Only special
fingerings are included. All others are
executed with regular fingerings.

PIANISSIMO FINGERINGS

Often, students find playing notes in the c^3 and c^4 range difficult. This is a result of the principle that the higher the note, the less air needed to produce the tone. These tones become increasingly more difficult when the composer places the added demands of pianissimo markings on the manuscript. To play soft in the upper register means even less air going into the instrument causing many of the notes to be played flat. Since many solos end with a high pianissimo note, the following pianissimo fingerings are provided to assist the performer. These fingerings are slightly sharp and should be used only upon sustained pianissimo tones to counteract the natural tendency of these tones to sound flat when played softly. These fingerings are especially helpful in solo playing.

APPENDIX G

LIST OF FLUTE MANUFACTURING COMPANIES

1. Almeida Flutes, Arrowhead Drive, Tiverton, Rhode Island.

2. Armstrong Company, Inc., 1000 Industrial Parkway, Elkhart, Indiana.

3. Artley, Inc., 616 Enterprise Drive, Oak Brook, Illinois.

4. Artley West, Inc., 1 Artley Drive, Box 2280, Nogales, Arizona.

5. Coll Divine Flutes, Box 734, San Antonio, Texas.

6. DeFord Co., Box 865, Elkart, Indiana.

7. Emerson Flutes, 28135 West Hively, Elkhart, Indiana.

8. Fredricks Flutes and Piccolos, 1414 South Main Street, Royal Oak, Michigan.

9. Gemeinhardt Co., Box 788, Elkhart, Indiana.

10. Haynes Flute Co., 12 Piedmont Street, Boston, Massachusetts.

11. King Musical Instruments, Inc., 33999 Curtis Blvd., Eastlake, Ohio.

12. Landoll Flutes, R.F.D.#1, Arlington, Vermont.

13. Mateki Flutes, 653 Alto Drive, Pittsburgh, Pa.

14. Miyazawa Flutes, P. O. Box 5521, 1214 5th Street, Coralville, Iowa.

15. Muramatsu Flutes, 1414 South Main St., Royal Oak, Michigan.

16. Pearl Flutes, P. O. Box 909, Sun Valley, California.

17. Powell Flutes, Inc., 70 Bow Street, Arlington Heights, Massachusetts.

18. Prima Sankyo Flutes, 2525 East Douglas, Wichita, Kansas.

19. Reynolds and Son, Inc., 3404 Waterview Road, Dallas, Texas.

20. Yamaha Musical Instruments, 6600 Orangethorpe, Box 6600, Buena Park, California.

For a more complete list of additional companies that not only manufacture flutes but also supply various products or services useful to school music programs, consult the Music Industry Catalog, 1978-79, "Master List of Companies," pp. 7-18, published by the Instrumentalist Company, 1418 Lake Street, Evanston, Illinois 60204.

RECOMMENDED COLLATERAL READING

Acoustics

Backus, John. The Acoustical Foundation of Music. New York: W. W. Norton, 1972.

Bartholemew, Wilmer. Acoustics of Music. New York: Prentice Hall, 1946.

Benade, A. H. Fundamentals of Musical Acoustics. London: Oxford University Press, 1976.

Culver, Charles A. Musical Acoustics. New York: McGraw Hill, 1956.

Erickson, Robert. Sound Structure in Music. Berkley: University of California Press, 1975.

Fletcher, Neville. "Some Acoustical Principles of Flute Technique," Instrumentalist, 28:7, February 1974, pp. 57-62.

Nederveen, Cornelius. Acoustical Aspects of Woodwind Instruments. Amsterdam: Frits Knuf, 1969.

Rigden, John. Physics and the Sound of Music. New York: John Wiley and Son, 1972.

Contemporary

Bartolozzi, Bruno. New Sounds for Woodwinds. London: Oxford University Press, 1967.

Cage, John. Notations. New York: Something Else Press, 1909.

Cope, David. "Contemporary Notation in Music," Instrumentalist, 30:10, May 1976, pp. 28-32.

Howell, Thomas. The Avant-Garde Flute: A Handbook for Composers and Flutists. Berkley: University of California Press, 1974.

Read, Gardner. Contemporary Instrumental Technique. New York: Schirmer Books, 1976.

Risatti, Howard. New Music Vocabulary: A Guide to Notational Signs for Contemporary Music. Chicago: University of Illinois Press, 1975.

Stokes, Sheridon and Richard Condon. Special Effects for Flute. California: Trio Associates, 1972.

Fingerings

Arnold, Jay. Modern Fingering System for Flute. New York: Shapiro, Bernstein and Co., 1963.

Pellerite, James. A Modern Guide to Fingerings for the Flute.
Indiana: Zalo Publications, 1972.

General

Boehm, Theobald. The Flute and Flute Playing. New York: Dover
Press, 1964.

Carse, Adam. Musical Wind Instruments. New York: Da Capo
Press, 1965.

DeLaney, Charles. Teacher's Guide to the Flute. Elkhart,
Indiana: Selmer Co., n.d.

LeJeune, Harriet. A Flutist's Manual. Evanston, Illinois:
Summy-Birchard Co., 1964.

Quantz, Johann. On Playing Flute. New York: Schirmer and Co.,
1976.

Timm, Everett. The Woodwinds. Boston: Allyn and Bacon, 1964.

Weerts, Richard. Handbook for Woodwinds. Kirksville, Missouri:
Simpson Publishing Co., 1966.

History

Baines, Anthony. Woodwind Instruments and Their History. New
York: W. W. Norton, 1957.

Galpin, Francis. A Textbook of European Musical Instruments:
Their Origin, History and Character. New York: J. DeGroff,
1956.

Geiringer, Karl. Musical Instruments, Their History in Western
Culture. New York: Oxford University Press, 1945.

Sachs, Curt. The History of Musical Instruments. New York: W.
W. Norton, 1940.

Instrument Repair

Brand, Erick. Band Instrument Repair Manual. Elkhart, Indiana:
Erick Brand, 1946.

Springer, George H. Maintenance and Repair of Wind and Percussion
Instruments. Boston: Allyn and Bacon, 1976.

Teide, Clayton. The Practical Band Instrumental Repair Manual.
Dubuque, Iowa: William C. Brown, Pub., 1976.

Weissar, Otto. Preventive Maintenance of Musical Instruments.
New York: Belwin, Inc., 1972.

Literature

Kujala, Walfrid. "New Solo and Study Materials for Flute."
Instrumentalist, 32:7, February 1978, pp. 50-53.

Pellerite, James. A Handbook of Literature for the Flute. Indiana: Zalo Publications, 1978.

Vester, Frans. Flute Repertoire Catalogue. London: Musica Rara, 1967.

Wilkins, Frederick. A Catalog of Music Literature for the Flute. Arizona: Artley Inc., n.d.

Wilkins, Wayne. General Catalogue of Flute Music. California: Trio Assoc., n.d.

Wilkins, Wayne. The Index of Flute Music. Arkansas: The Music Register, 1974.

Technique

Abbott, Deborah. "Rule of Tongue: Tips for Slips of the Trade." Selmer Band Wagon, No. 71, 1975, pp. 29-31.

Chapman, F. B. Flute Technique. London: Oxford University Press, 1936.

Dehaney, Charles. "An Approach to Flute Vibrato through Listening and Playing," Selmer Band Wagon, No. 85, 1978, pp. 8-9.

Dick, Robert. The Other Flute: A Performance Manual of Technique. New York: Oxford University Press, 1975.

Goodbert, Robert. "A Long Tone Exercise for Flutists," Instrumentalist, 30:3, October, 1975, pp. 46-51.

Hahn, Richard. "The Flute and the Soda Straw," Instrumentalist, 30:3, October 1975, pp. 46-51.

Karkoschka, Erhard. Notation in Music, A Critical Guide to Interpretation and Realization. New York: Praeger, 1972.

Keller, Hermann. Phrasing and Articulation. New York: W. W. Norton, 1965.

Palmer, Harold. Teaching Technique of the Woodwinds. New York: Belwin Co., 1952.

Porter, Maurice M. The Embouchure. London: Boosey and Hawkes, 1967.

Sigurdson, Gary. "The Importance of Intonation." Conn Chord, 18:2, Fall 1974, pp. 14-15.

BIBLIOGRAPHY

Abbott, Deborah. "Rule of Tongue: Tips for Slips of the Trade,"
    Selmer Band Wagon, No. 71, 1975, pp. 29-31.

Andrews, Ralph. "Problems of the Peripatetic Piccolo Person,"
    DeFord Digest, April 1976, pp. 3-4.

Backus, John. The Acoustical Foundation of Music.
    New York: W. W. Norton, 1972.

Baines, Anthony. Woodwind Instruments and Their History.
    New York: W. W. Norton, 1957.

Bartholemew, Wilmer. Acoustics of Music.
    New York: Prentice Hall, 1946.

Bartolozzi, Bruno. New Sounds for Woodwinds.
    London: Oxford Press, 1967.

Bennett, Harold, "A New Intonation Discovery,"
    Woodwind, November 1950, p. 6.

Boehm, Theobald. The Flute and Flute Playing.
    New York: Dover Press, 1964.

Brand, Erick. Band Instrument Repair Manual.
    Elkhart, Indiana: Eric Brand, 1946.

Brown, Carol. "Piccolo Solos,"
    Instrumentalist, 31:4, November 1976, pp. 50-54.

Cage, John. Notations.
    New York: Something Else Press, 1969.

Chapman, F. B. Flute Technique.
    London: Oxford University Press, 1936.

Cope, David. "Contemporary Notation in Music,"
    Instrumentalist, 30:10, May 1976, pp. 28-32.

Dameron, Jeanette. "Listen and Evaluate,"
    DeFord Digest, April 1975, p. 1.

DeLaney, Charles. "An Approach to Flute Vibrato through
    Listening and Playing," Selmer Band Wagon, No. 85, 1978,
    pp. 8-9.

Dick, Robert. The Other Flute: A Performance Manual of Technique.
    New York: Oxford, 1975.

Down, J. W. "Learning, Performing, and Teaching: Observations of
    a Flute Teacher," Instrumentalist, 33:10, May 1979, pp. 44-49.

Fajardo, Raoul. "Characteristics of the Flute Embouchure Hole."
    Instrumentalist, 30:4, November 1975, pp. 55-59.

215

Fletcher, Neville. "Some Acoustical Principles of Flute
    Technique," Instrumentalist, 28:7, February 1974, pp. 57-62.

Fletcher, Neville, "Acoustics of the Flute, Part I,"
    Instrumentalist, 27:6, January 1972, pp. 36-40.

Fletcher, Neville. "Acoustics of the Flute, Part II,"
    Instrumentalist, 27:7, February 1972, pp. 37-43.

Goodbert, Robert. "A Long Tone Exercise for Flutists,"
    Instrumentalist, 21:7, February 1977, pp. 56-60.

Gowman, Roy. "Selecting a Method Book for Beginners,"
    Instrumentalist, 32:1, August 1977, p. 26.

Hahn, Richard. "The Flute and the Soda Straw,"
    Instrumentalist, 30:3, October 1975, pp. 46-51.

Houston, Patricia. "Flute Intonation Tips for Band Directors,"
    Royal Notes, Spring 1978, p. 8.

Howell, Thomas. The Avant-Garde Flute: A Handbook for Composers
    and Flutists. Berkley: University of California Press, 1974.

Jones, William. "Some New Fingerings for Alto Flute,"
    Instrumentalist, 29:10, May 1975, pp. 47-48.

Jones, William. "The Alto Flute, Part I,"
    Instrumentalist, 33:5, December 1978, pp. 56-58.

Karkoschka, Erhard. Notation in Music. A Critical Guide to
    Interpretation and Realization. New York: Praeger, 1972.

Kniebusch, Carol. "Flute Choirs are the Answer,"
    Instrumentalist, 35:9, April 1981, pp. 32-36.

Kujala, Walfrid. "New Solo and Study Materials for Flute,"
    Instrumentalist, 32:7, February 1978, pp. 50-53.

Kuschick, Marilyn. "Practice Those Ever Lovin' Long Tones, Part I,"
    Instrumentalist, 32:3, October 1977, pp. 72-74.

Kuschick, Marilyn. "Doriot Anthony Dwyer, Boston's First Flutist,"
    Instrumentalist, 30:11, June 1977, pp. 40-44.

Mahin, Bruce. "20th Century Music Notation,"
    Instrumentalist, 36:7, February 1978, pp. 34-35.

Maher, Betty. "My Favorite Duets,"
    Instrumentalist, 28:4, November 1973, pp. 58-60.

Montgomery, William. "Flute Tone Production, Part I,"
    Instrumentalist, 33:2, September 1978, pp. 46-50.

Older, Julia. "Julius Baker on Tone and Technique, Notes from a
    Master Class," Instrumentalist, 30:9, April 1976, pp. 41-46.

Opperman, George, "The New Piccolo,"
    Woodwind, April 1951, p. 6.

Osborne, Charles. "Music for Young Flutists,"
    Royal Notes, Mid-Winter 1978, pp. 8-9.

Osborne, Charles. "Music for Young Flutists,"
    Royal Notes, Spring 1978, p. 10.

Osborne, Charles. "Selected Duets for Two Flutes: An Annotated
    Listing," DeFord Digest, September 1975, pp. 2-3.

Palmer, Harold. Teaching Techniques of the Woodwinds,
    New York: Belwin Co., 1952.

Pellerite, James J. A Handbook of Literature for the Flute.
    Indiana: Zalo Publications, 1978.

Porter, Dale. "More Than You Wish to Know about Intonation."
    DeFord Digest, April 1975, p. 1.

Read, Gardner. Contemporary Instructional Techniques.
    New York: Schirmer, 1976.

Rees, William. "New Music for the Flute Choir,"
    Instrumentalist, 31:8, March 1977, pp. 92-94.

Risatti, Howard. New Music Vocabulary: A Guide to Notational
    Signs for Contemporary Music. Chicago: University of
    Illinois Press, 1975.

Rose, Donna. "Spitting Seeds: Flute Tips Takahashi Style."
    Instrumentalist, 37:3, October 1982, pp. 32-35.

Sachs, Curt. The History of Musical Instruments.
    New York: W. W. Norton, 1940.

Sigurdson, Gary. "The Importance of Intonation,"
    Conn Chord, 18:2, Fall 1974, pp. 14-15.

Simpson, Mary Jean. "A Vibrant Tone for Everyone,"
    Instrumentalist, 30:2, September 1974, pp. 53-56.

Stone, Curt. "New Notation in Music,"
    Music Educator's Journal, 63:2, October 1976, pp. 48-56.

Timm, Everett. The Woodwinds.
    Boston: Allyn and Bacon, 1964.

Vester, Frans. Flute Repertoire Catalogue.
    London: Musica Rara, 1967.

Waln, Ronald. "The Flutist's Forte,"
    Instrumentalist, 29:9, April 1975, pp. 44-45.

Webb, Robert. "An Annotated Flute Choir Bibliography."
    Instrumentalist, 29:11, June 1975, pp. 63-67.

217

Weerts, Richard. Handbook for Woodwinds.
     Missouri: Simpson Publishing Co., 1966.

Westbrook, James. Do Flute Players Ever Warm Up,"
     Instrumentalist, 32:2, September 1977, pp. 60-64.

DR. THOMAS E. RAINEY, JR.

A recognized leading educator in flute, Dr. Thomas E. Rainey received his doctorate from the University of Pittsburgh. He also has earned a Bachelor of Music degree from Duquesne University, and a Masters of Music from Youngstown State University. Dr. Rainey has also studied at Connecticut and Morehead Schools of Music. He has studied with such renowned musicians as Bernard Goldberg, Eugene Rousseau, Walter Mayhall, Joseph Mariano, John Wummer, Danti DiThomas, John LaPorta, Jerry Coker, and Nathan Davis. A man of many talents, he is well versed in both the jazz and classical fields.

Thomas Rainey has gained wide recognition both in the areas of music education and performance. He has been actively involved in public school teaching, instructor of flute at the university level, master flute classes, symphony work, jazz improvization courses, woodwind quintets, adjudicator, woodwind methods courses, jazz bands, and private instruction. He has held several offices in his state music education associations. In addition, Dr. Rainey has written numerous educational articles. He is listed in the "International Who's Who Among Musicians".

223